The art of direct selling guide

The Beginner's Guide to Mastering Direct Selling

Rowan Blake

Table of Contents

Introduction

Overview of direct selling and its benefits

Direct selling is a unique business model that has been gaining popularity in recent years, and for good reason. This model involves selling products directly to consumers, without the need for a middleman. It allows individuals to start their own businesses and become entrepreneurs, while also providing customers with a more personal shopping experience.

One of the key benefits of direct selling is that it allows individuals to be their own boss. They have the freedom to set their own schedule, work from home, and choose which products they want to sell. This level of independence and flexibility is incredibly appealing to many people, especially those who are looking for a way to earn extra income or start a business on their own terms.

Direct selling also provides a low-cost entry point into entrepreneurship. Unlike traditional businesses, which often require significant upfront investments in inventory, storefronts, and other expenses, direct selling businesses typically have low startup costs. This means that individuals can start selling products with little to no overhead, and focus on building their customer base and generating income.

Another key benefit of direct selling is the opportunity for personal growth and development. As individuals build their businesses, they have the chance to learn new skills, such as sales and marketing, time management, and leadership. They also have the opportunity to connect with like-minded individuals and build a community of support and encouragement.

Direct selling also provides a more personal shopping experience for customers. Instead of purchasing products from a big box store or online retailer, customers can work directly with a representative who can answer their questions, make recommendations, and provide personalized service. This level of customer service is often hard to find in traditional retail settings, and it can make a big difference in customer satisfaction and loyalty.

In addition to these benefits, direct selling also has a positive impact on the economy. It creates jobs and opportunities for individuals who may not have access to traditional employment, such as stay-at-home parents or individuals with disabilities. It also supports small businesses and promotes entrepreneurship, which are essential components of a healthy economy.

Despite all of these benefits, direct selling is not without its challenges. It requires hard work, dedication, and persistence to build a successful business. Individuals must be willing to invest time and effort into building their customer base, developing their skills, and overcoming obstacles along the way.

However, for those who are willing to put in the work, direct selling can be an incredibly rewarding and fulfilling business model. It provides individuals with the opportunity to take control of their financial future, build their own businesses, and make a positive impact on the lives of others.

Direct selling is a unique and powerful business model that offers many benefits for individuals and the economy as a whole. It provides individuals with the opportunity to be their own boss, start a business with low startup costs, and develop new skills and connections. It also provides customers with a more personal shopping experience and supports small businesses and entrepreneurship. While direct selling is not without its challenges, it is a worthwhile and rewarding pursuit for those who are willing to put in the work.

The role of direct selling in the business world is multifaceted and continues to evolve. It provides a means of income for individuals, a powerful tool for companies, and a personal connection between the salesperson and the customer. It also has a significant impact on the economy and has the potential to reach niche markets that may not be reached through traditional retail channels. While there are challenges associated with direct selling, the benefits it provides make it a valuable and important part of the business world.

Chapter One

The Basics of Direct Selling
Defining direct selling and its different forms

Direct selling is a form of marketing that has been in existence for centuries. It is a process whereby a company sells products or services directly to the consumers without involving intermediaries such as retailers, wholesalers, or middlemen. Direct selling can be conducted through various channels, including face-to-face, online, or over the phone. It is a versatile marketing technique that offers a wide range of benefits to both the companies and consumers.

One of the primary benefits of direct selling is that it enables companies to establish a more personal relationship with their customers. By eliminating intermediaries, companies can interact directly with their consumers, which enables them to understand their needs and preferences better. This, in turn, enables them to tailor their products and services to meet the specific needs of their customers, which can enhance customer satisfaction and loyalty.

Another benefit of direct selling is that it provides a more cost-effective method of selling products and services. By eliminating intermediaries, companies can save on distribution costs, such as transportation, warehousing, and advertising, which can reduce the overall cost of the products. This, in turn, enables them to offer their products and services at a more competitive price, which can attract more customers.

Direct selling can take different forms, including party plan selling, network marketing, and one-to-one selling. Party plan selling is a type of direct selling that involves organizing home parties or demonstrations to promote and sell products. It is a social and interactive selling technique that enables customers to try out products before they buy them. Party plan selling is particularly suitable for products that require demonstration, such as cosmetics, kitchenware, and home décor.

Network marketing, also known as multi-level marketing (MLM), is a type of direct selling that involves building a network of distributors who sell products and recruit others to do the same. In network marketing, distributors earn a commission on their sales and the sales of their recruits. This creates a win-win situation for the company and the distributors since the company can expand its sales force, while the distributors can earn an income by selling products and recruiting others.

One-to-one selling, also known as person-to-person selling, is a type of direct selling that involves selling products and services directly to individuals. It is a personalized selling technique that enables companies to establish a more personal relationship with their customers. One-to-one selling is particularly suitable for products that require a high degree of personalization, such as clothing, jewelry, and accessories.

Direct selling is a versatile and effective marketing technique that offers a wide range of benefits to both companies and consumers. By eliminating intermediaries, direct selling enables companies to establish a more personal relationship with their customers, which can enhance customer satisfaction and loyalty. It also provides a more cost-effective method of selling products and services, which can reduce the overall cost of the products and attract more customers. Direct selling can take different forms, including party plan selling, network marketing, and one-to-one selling, each of which has its unique advantages and disadvantages. In the next chapter, we will explore the direct selling process and how it works.

Understanding the direct selling process

Direct selling is a unique business model that has gained popularity over the years. It involves selling products directly to consumers through personal contact rather than through retail establishments. In this chapter, we will explore the direct selling process, the steps involved, and how it differs from other sales methods.

At its core, direct selling is about building relationships. A direct seller establishes a personal connection with a potential customer, educating them about the products and creating a sense of trust. The seller acts as an ambassador for the brand, promoting its values and benefits to the customer.

The direct selling process involves several steps. The first step is to identify potential customers and establish contact with them. This can be done through referrals, networking, or through social media. Once contact has been established, the seller will provide information about the products and answer any questions the customer may have.

The next step is to provide a demonstration of the product. This can be done in person or online, depending on the product and the customer's preference. The demonstration should showcase the product's features and benefits and highlight how it can solve the customer's problem.

After the demonstration, the seller should follow up with the customer to gauge their interest and address any remaining concerns. If the customer is interested in purchasing the product, the seller can close the sale by providing instructions for payment and delivery.

One of the benefits of direct selling is that it allows the seller to establish a relationship with the customer that extends beyond the initial sale. The seller can provide ongoing support, answer questions, and provide additional product information as needed. This can lead to repeat business and referrals, which are key to building a successful direct selling business.

Direct selling differs from traditional retail sales in several ways. Unlike retail sales, direct selling is often done in a one-on-one setting, allowing the seller to provide personalized attention to the customer. Additionally, direct selling often involves a demonstration of the product, allowing the customer to see and experience the product firsthand.

Direct selling also offers benefits to the seller. For one, it provides a flexible work schedule that can be tailored to the seller's needs. Direct selling can be done full-time or part-time, allowing the seller to earn additional income while pursuing other interests or obligations.

Another benefit of direct selling is that it allows the seller to be their own boss. Direct sellers are responsible for their own success and can choose their own approach to selling and promoting products. This can be empowering and allows the seller to take control of their financial future.

There are several different forms of direct selling, including party plan, network marketing, and person-to-person selling. Party plan involves hosting a gathering or party where the seller showcases the products and encourages guests to make purchases. Network marketing involves recruiting others to become sellers, creating a network of sellers who work together to promote the products. Person-to-person selling involves direct contact with potential customers, either in person or through social media.

The direct selling process involves establishing a personal connection with potential customers, providing information and demonstrations of the product, and following up to close the sale. Direct selling offers several benefits to both the seller and the customer, including personalized attention and flexibility. Understanding the different forms of direct selling can help sellers choose the approach that works best for them and their business.

Advantages and disadvantages of direct selling

Direct selling has been gaining popularity over the years, and it's not hard to see why. This business model offers a number of advantages that are attractive to both entrepreneurs and consumers. However, like any other business model, direct selling also has its own set of disadvantages that must be considered. In this section, we will discuss the advantages and disadvantages of direct selling.

Advantages of Direct Selling:

1. Flexibility: One of the biggest advantages of direct selling is the flexibility it offers. As a direct seller, you can choose your own schedule and work from anywhere, making it a great option for those who value work-life balance.

2. Low start-up costs: Direct selling businesses require minimal start-up costs compared to traditional businesses. This makes it a great option for those who want to start a business but don't have a lot of capital to invest.

3. Personal touch: Direct selling allows you to build personal relationships with your customers, which can lead to greater customer loyalty and satisfaction. By providing personalized service, you can differentiate yourself from other businesses and build a loyal customer base.

4. Unlimited income potential: Direct selling offers unlimited income potential. As a direct seller, your income is based on your sales and the sales of your team. With hard work and dedication, you can earn a substantial income.

5. Training and support: Direct selling companies often provide training and support to their sellers, which can help them succeed in their business. This support can range from product training to business development coaching.

Disadvantages of Direct Selling:

1. High competition: Direct selling can be highly competitive, with many other sellers vying for the same customers. This can make it difficult to stand out and attract new customers.

2. Sales pressure: Direct selling requires a lot of salesmanship and persuasion skills. Sellers may feel pressure to make sales and meet quotas, which can be stressful and can lead to burnout.

3. Limited market: Direct selling is often limited to a specific geographic area, which can limit the potential customer base. This can make it difficult to expand the business and increase sales.

4. Dependence on the company: Direct sellers are dependent on the company for their products and support. If the company experiences financial difficulties or goes out of business, the seller's business can be negatively impacted.

5. Negative perception: Direct selling has historically had a negative perception due to the actions of some unscrupulous sellers. This can make it difficult for legitimate sellers to gain the trust of potential customers.

Overall, direct selling offers many advantages for entrepreneurs looking to start their own business. However, it's important to consider the potential disadvantages and challenges as well. By carefully weighing the pros and cons of direct selling and developing a solid business plan, entrepreneurs can build a successful and profitable direct selling business.

Chapter Two

Setting Up Your Direct Selling Business
Choosing the right direct selling company

Choosing the right direct selling company is a crucial step for any aspiring direct seller. With countless companies vying for attention, it can be overwhelming to determine which one is the best fit for you. However, with careful consideration and research, you can find the right company that aligns with your values, goals, and interests.

First and foremost, it's important to assess the products or services that the company offers. Are they unique and innovative? Are they of high quality? Are they products that you yourself would use and recommend to others? These are important questions to ask when evaluating a direct selling company. You want to be passionate about what you're selling, and you want to be confident that the products are something that your potential customers will want to purchase.

Another key factor to consider is the compensation plan. Look closely at the commission structure and incentives that the company offers. How much commission will you earn per sale? Are there bonuses or other incentives for achieving certain sales goals? It's important to fully understand the compensation plan to determine if it aligns with your financial goals and expectations.

The company's reputation is also critical when choosing a direct selling company. Research the company online and read reviews from other direct sellers and customers. Look for any red flags or complaints about the company's practices or products. If a company has a history of unethical behavior or a poor reputation, it's best to steer clear.

It's also important to assess the level of support and training that the company provides. As a new direct seller, you will likely need guidance and support to build your business. Look for a company that offers training programs, resources, and ongoing support to help you succeed. The company's leadership and culture should also be taken into consideration. Are they accessible and supportive? Do they promote a positive and collaborative atmosphere?

Legal considerations are also important when choosing a direct selling company. Look for a company that is compliant with the relevant laws and regulations in your country or region. The company should provide clear and transparent information about their business practices, compensation plan, and product claims. Avoid companies that make unrealistic or exaggerated claims about their products or earnings potential.

Finally, consider your personal values and interests when choosing a direct selling company. Look for a company that aligns with your values and beliefs. If you're passionate about health and wellness, for example, look for a company that offers health-related products. If you're interested in sustainability, look for a company that prioritizes environmentally friendly practices. When you're passionate about what you're selling, it will be easier to connect with customers and build a successful business.

Choosing the right direct selling company is a crucial step in building a successful direct selling business. Consider the products, compensation plan, reputation, support and training, legal considerations, and personal values when evaluating potential companies. With careful consideration and research, you can find the right company that aligns with your goals and helps you build a thriving business.

Setting goals and creating a business plan

In the world of direct selling, setting goals and creating a solid business plan are essential for success. Without clear objectives and a roadmap to achieve them, a direct selling business can quickly flounder and fail to gain traction. Therefore, it is critical to take the time to develop a well-defined business plan that outlines your goals, strategies, and tactics.

The first step in setting goals for your direct selling business is to identify what you want to achieve. Are you looking to build a customer base, recruit a team of sales representatives, or both? Perhaps you have a specific revenue target in mind or a particular product line that you want to focus on. Whatever your goals may be, they should be specific, measurable, and achievable.

Once you have identified your goals, the next step is to develop a plan to achieve them. This is where a business plan comes into play. A good business plan should include a detailed description of your products or services, your target market, your competition, and your marketing strategy. It should also outline your financial projections, including your revenue goals and expenses.

When developing your business plan, it is important to be realistic about your goals and projections. While it's great to be optimistic and ambitious, setting unrealistic goals can lead to disappointment and frustration. Additionally, you should always have a contingency plan in place in case things don't go as expected.

In order to create a successful business plan, it's important to conduct thorough market research. This will help you identify your target market and understand their needs and preferences. It will also help you evaluate your competition and determine how you can differentiate yourself from them.

Another key element of a business plan is your marketing strategy. This should include a detailed plan for promoting your products or services, including your pricing strategy, distribution channels, and advertising tactics. You should also consider how you will use social media and other online platforms to reach potential customers.

Finally, your business plan should include financial projections, including your revenue goals and expenses. This will help you determine how much money you need to invest in your business and how long it will take to achieve your goals. You should also consider the potential risks and challenges that could impact your business and how you will mitigate them.

In addition to setting goals and creating a business plan, it is important to monitor your progress and adjust your strategies as needed. This means regularly reviewing your financial projections and marketing efforts and making adjustments based on your results.

Setting goals and creating a solid business plan are critical to the success of a direct selling business. By taking the time to develop a well-defined plan that outlines your goals, strategies, and tactics, you can position yourself for success and achieve the results you desire. However, it is important to be realistic and flexible, and to monitor your progress closely in order to make adjustments as needed.

Legal considerations for direct sellers

When it comes to direct selling, there are certain legal considerations that sellers must keep in mind in order to avoid potential legal issues and protect their business. In this section, we will explore some of the key legal considerations that direct sellers should be aware of.

First and foremost, it is important to note that direct sellers are typically considered independent contractors rather than employees. This means that they are responsible for their own taxes and must comply with all relevant tax laws and regulations. Direct sellers should keep detailed records of all income and expenses related to their business and may need to file quarterly estimated tax payments in order to avoid penalties.

Another important legal consideration for direct sellers is compliance with state and federal laws related to direct selling. In the United States, the Federal Trade Commission (FTC) regulates the direct selling industry and has established rules to protect consumers from unfair or deceptive practices. Direct sellers must comply with these rules, which include providing accurate and truthful information about their products and business opportunity, providing a written disclosure statement to potential recruits, and offering a reasonable buyback policy for unsold inventory.

In addition to complying with FTC rules, direct sellers must also be aware of state-specific laws related to direct selling. For example, some states require direct sellers to obtain a license or registration in order to operate legally. Direct sellers should research the laws in their state and ensure that they are in compliance.

Intellectual property is another important legal consideration for direct sellers. Direct sellers may be selling products that are protected by patents, trademarks, or copyrights, and it is important to ensure that they have the legal right to sell these products. Direct sellers should also be aware of their own intellectual property rights, such as trademarks or logos, and take steps to protect them.

Privacy and data security are also important considerations for direct sellers. Direct sellers often collect personal information from their customers and recruits, such as names, addresses, and credit card information. It is important to ensure that this information is kept secure and that privacy policies are in place to protect customer data.

Direct sellers should also be aware of advertising and marketing laws and regulations. Direct sellers should ensure that all advertising and marketing materials are truthful and not deceptive. This includes avoiding making false or exaggerated claims about products or income potential.

Finally, direct sellers should be aware of any contractual agreements that they enter into with their direct selling company. These agreements may include terms related to compensation, termination, and non-compete clauses. Direct sellers should carefully review these agreements and seek legal advice if necessary to ensure that they fully understand the terms and their legal obligations.

There are a number of legal considerations that direct sellers must keep in mind in order to operate their business legally and avoid potential legal issues. Compliance with state and federal laws, protection of intellectual property, data privacy and security, advertising and marketing regulations, and contractual agreements are all important factors that direct sellers should be aware of. By taking the time to understand and comply with these legal considerations, direct sellers can protect their business and build a solid foundation for long-term success.

Chapter Three

Product Knowledge and Marketing
Product research and knowledge

In the world of direct selling, having a deep understanding of the products or services that you are offering to customers is crucial for your success. After all, customers are more likely to purchase a product from someone who knows what they are talking about and can provide valuable information about the benefits and features of the product.

Product research is the process of gathering information about a particular product or service, analyzing that information, and using it to make informed decisions. As a direct seller, your product knowledge and research skills can make or break your business.

The first step in product research is to know your audience. Who are you selling to, and what do they want or need? Understanding your target market will help you determine what products or services to offer, and how to market them effectively.

Once you have identified your target market, it's time to start researching your products. This involves gathering as much information as possible about the product, including its features, benefits, pricing, and competitors. You can do this by visiting the manufacturer's website, attending product training sessions, reading product reviews, and conducting your own product tests.

When researching your products, it's important to focus on the features and benefits that are most relevant to your customers. For example, if you are selling skincare products, you might focus on the anti-aging benefits of the products for older customers, or the acne-fighting benefits for younger customers. By tailoring your product knowledge to your target market, you can more effectively sell your products and build customer loyalty.

Another important aspect of product research is keeping up with industry trends. This involves staying informed about new product releases, changes in customer preferences, and emerging technologies that could impact your business. By staying on top of industry trends, you can identify new product opportunities, adapt to changing customer needs, and stay ahead of the competition.

In addition to product research, effective direct selling also requires a strong understanding of marketing. Once you have a deep understanding of your products and target market, you can develop a marketing plan that will help you reach potential customers and drive sales.

Your marketing plan should include a clear message that communicates the unique benefits of your products or services, as well as the key features that differentiate them from the competition. You should also consider the best channels to reach your target audience, such as social media, email marketing, or in-person events.

Branding is also an important part of marketing. This involves creating a distinct identity for your business that communicates your values and mission to customers. A strong brand can help build customer loyalty, differentiate you from the competition, and make it easier to sell your products.

Overall, product research and marketing are critical components of successful direct selling. By investing time and energy into understanding your products and target market, and developing a comprehensive marketing plan, you can build a profitable direct selling business and achieve your goals.

Creating a marketing plan for your direct selling business

Marketing is a crucial aspect of any business, including direct selling. In order to achieve success in the world of direct selling, it is important to create a solid marketing plan that will help you reach your target audience and drive sales. A marketing plan is a strategic roadmap that outlines the various tactics you will use to promote your products or services to potential customers. It is a crucial component of any direct selling business, as it can help you to differentiate your products from those of your competitors and build a strong brand identity.

The first step in creating a marketing plan for your direct selling business is to define your target market. This involves identifying the specific group of people who are most likely to be interested in your products or services. Once you have a clear understanding of your target audience, you can begin to develop messaging that will resonate with them and appeal to their needs and interests.

One effective strategy for marketing your direct selling business is to leverage social media platforms. Social media has become an increasingly important channel for reaching customers, and it offers a range of tools and features that can help you to build your brand and promote your products. By creating engaging content that speaks to your target audience, you can increase your visibility and drive traffic to your website or sales pages.

Another key component of your marketing plan should be email marketing. Email marketing is a powerful tool for building relationships with customers and nurturing leads. By creating targeted email campaigns that speak to the specific needs and interests of your audience, you can encourage them to take action and make a purchase.

In addition to these tactics, it is also important to consider traditional marketing methods, such as advertising and public relations. Advertising can help you to reach a wider audience and raise awareness of your brand, while public relations can help you to build credibility and establish yourself as an authority in your industry.

Ultimately, the key to creating a successful marketing plan for your direct selling business is to be strategic and intentional. By taking the time to understand your target audience, develop compelling messaging, and choose the right marketing channels, you can build a strong brand identity and drive sales. With the right marketing plan in place, you can achieve success in the world of direct selling and take your business to the next level.

Branding and positioning your business in the market

Branding and positioning are crucial aspects of any business, including direct selling. As a direct seller, it's essential to establish your brand and position it effectively in the market to gain a competitive edge.

Branding is about creating an identity for your business. It includes designing a unique logo, selecting a color palette, and creating a tagline that communicates the essence of your business. Your brand should represent your values, mission, and vision.

Positioning, on the other hand, refers to the process of creating a unique space in the market that sets your business apart from the competition. It involves identifying the unique selling points of your product or service and using them to differentiate your business from others.

To effectively brand and position your direct selling business, there are several steps you should take:

1. Identify Your Unique Selling Proposition (USP)
   Your USP is what sets your product or service apart from others in the market. To determine your USP, you need

to understand your target audience's needs, preferences, and pain points. Once you have identified these factors, you can create a product or service that meets those needs and offers a unique solution.

2. Create a Compelling Brand Story
   Your brand story is what connects your audience to your business emotionally. It's the narrative that communicates your values, mission, and vision. Your brand story should be authentic, relatable, and memorable.

3. Design a Memorable Logo and Visual Identity
   Your logo and visual identity are essential components of your brand. They should be memorable, unique, and easily recognizable. A professional graphic designer can help you create a logo and visual identity that reflects your brand's personality.

4. Develop a Consistent Tone of Voice
   Your brand's tone of voice is how you communicate with your audience. It should be consistent across all your marketing materials and reflect your brand's personality. A consistent tone of voice helps to establish your brand's identity and builds trust with your audience.

5. Leverage Social Media
   Social media is an essential tool for branding and positioning your direct selling business. Platforms like Facebook, Twitter, Instagram, and LinkedIn allow you to

connect with your audience and share your brand story. It's crucial to use these platforms effectively and consistently to build your brand and position your business in the market.

6. Offer Exceptional Customer Service
   Your customers are the foundation of your business. Offering exceptional customer service is essential for building brand loyalty and positioning your business as a reliable and trustworthy source. Make sure to respond promptly to customer inquiries, provide clear and concise information, and go above and beyond to exceed their expectations.

7. Monitor Your Brand's Reputation
   Your brand's reputation is crucial to your business's success. Make sure to monitor your brand's online reputation by setting up Google Alerts and monitoring social media channels for mentions of your brand. Respond promptly to any negative comments or reviews and take steps to address any issues that arise.

Branding and positioning are critical aspects of any business, including direct selling. By identifying your unique selling proposition, creating a compelling brand story, designing a memorable logo and visual identity, developing a consistent tone of voice, leveraging social media, offering exceptional customer service, and monitoring your brand's reputation, you can effectively brand and position your direct selling business in the market and gain a competitive edge.

Chapter Four

Sales Techniques for Direct Selling
Building relationships with customers

Building relationships with customers is crucial for any business, and this is especially true for direct selling businesses. In this type of business, your customers are not just people who buy your products, but they are also potential partners and advocates for your brand.

The first step in building relationships with customers is to understand their needs and preferences. This can be done through market research, surveys, and customer feedback. By understanding your customers' needs, you can tailor your products and services to meet those needs, which will make them more likely to purchase from you and recommend your business to others.

Another important aspect of building relationships with customers is to provide excellent customer service. This means being responsive to their inquiries and concerns, providing timely and accurate information, and going above and beyond to make sure they are satisfied with their purchase. By providing great customer service, you can build trust and loyalty with your customers, which can lead to repeat business and referrals.

It is also important to establish a personal connection with your customers. This can be done through personalized emails, phone calls, and follow-up messages. By reaching out to your customers on a personal level, you can show that you care about their satisfaction and are willing to go the extra mile to ensure it.

Another effective way to build relationships with customers is to offer incentives and rewards for their loyalty. This can include exclusive discounts, early access to new products, and special promotions. By offering these rewards, you can show your customers that you value their business and want to reward them for their loyalty.

Social media is also a powerful tool for building relationships with customers. By creating engaging content and interacting with your followers, you can create a community of loyal customers who are passionate about your brand. This can also help you reach new customers through social sharing and word-of-mouth marketing.

In addition to building relationships with individual customers, it is also important to build relationships with other businesses and organizations in your industry. This can include networking with other direct selling companies, attending industry conferences and events, and collaborating with other businesses on joint marketing initiatives.

Finally, it is important to remember that building relationships with customers is an ongoing process. It requires consistent effort and a genuine commitment to meeting their needs and providing exceptional service. By prioritizing customer relationships in your business strategy, you can create a loyal customer base that will help drive your business forward and support your growth over the long-term.

Effective communication in direct selling

Effective communication is a vital component in direct selling. It is the key to developing a relationship of trust and credibility with your potential customers. As a direct seller, you need to communicate effectively with your customers to persuade them to make a purchase. In this article, we'll take a closer look at how you can master the art of communication in direct selling.

The first step to effective communication is to understand your audience. Before you start selling, take some time to research and analyze your potential customers. What are their needs, desires, and pain points? What motivates them to buy? By understanding your target audience, you can tailor your communication to meet their specific needs.

Once you have a good understanding of your audience, the next step is to communicate your message in a clear and concise manner. Avoid using industry jargon or technical terms that your customers might not understand. Instead, use simple language that is easy to comprehend. Make sure that your message is relevant, concise, and informative. Be prepared to answer any questions that your customers may have and be patient in explaining complex concepts.

Non-verbal communication is also essential in direct selling. Your body language, facial expressions, and tone of voice can have a significant impact on how your customers perceive you. Be confident, maintain eye contact, and smile to create a positive impression. Use a friendly tone of voice and avoid speaking too fast or too slow. Pay attention to your customer's body language and adjust your communication style accordingly.

Another key aspect of effective communication in direct selling is active listening. Listening to your customers is essential to building a relationship of trust and understanding. When your customer is speaking, pay attention to what they are saying and give them your full attention. Avoid interrupting or cutting them off mid-sentence. Show that you are listening by nodding your head, repeating back key points, and asking clarifying questions.

In addition to active listening, it's also important to show empathy towards your customers. Empathy involves putting yourself in your customer's shoes and understanding their perspective. By showing empathy, you can create a connection with your customer and build a relationship based on trust and understanding.

The final key to effective communication in direct selling is follow-up. Follow-up involves staying in touch with your customers after the sale to ensure that they are satisfied with their purchase. It also involves keeping them informed of any new products or promotions that might interest them. By following up with your customers, you can build a long-term relationship with them and turn them into loyal repeat customers.

Effective communication is a vital component of direct selling. By understanding your audience, communicating your message clearly and concisely, using non-verbal communication, active listening, empathy, and follow-up, you can build a relationship of trust and credibility with your customers. With effective communication, you can persuade your customers to make a purchase and turn them into loyal, repeat customers.

Closing the sale and follow-up strategies

In the world of direct selling, closing the sale is the ultimate goal. However, it's not always as simple as presenting the product and waiting for the customer to say "yes." In fact, it's often the follow-up strategies that make all the difference in whether or not a sale is made.

The first step in closing the sale is to understand the customer's needs and wants. This requires active listening, asking questions, and empathizing with the customer's situation. By doing so, you can tailor your sales pitch to address their specific needs and show them how your product can solve their problems or improve their life.

Next, it's important to be confident and assertive in your approach. You need to demonstrate your expertise in the product and your ability to provide excellent customer service. This can be done through your tone of voice, body language, and the way you present your product.

One effective strategy for closing the sale is to offer a limited-time promotion or discount. This can create a sense of urgency and incentivize the customer to make a purchase now rather than later. However, it's important to make sure the promotion is genuine and not just a sales tactic, as customers can often see through insincerity.

Another effective technique is to use social proof. This involves sharing success stories or testimonials from satisfied customers who have already purchased the product. Seeing that others have had positive experiences can build trust and credibility with potential customers.

Once the sale is made, it's important to follow up with the customer to ensure their satisfaction and address any concerns they may have. This can be done through a phone call, email, or even a handwritten note. By showing that you care about their experience and value their business, you can build a long-term relationship with the customer and increase the likelihood of repeat sales.

Follow-up strategies can also include offering additional support or resources to the customer, such as instructional videos or tips on how to best use the product. This not only helps the customer get the most out of their purchase but also shows that you are invested in their success and satisfaction.

It's important to remember that closing the sale is not the end of the process. In fact, it's just the beginning of a long-term relationship with the customer. By focusing on follow-up strategies and building a strong relationship with the customer, you can not only increase the likelihood of repeat sales but also turn them into loyal brand ambassadors who will recommend your product to others.

Closing the sale in direct selling requires a combination of effective communication, confidence, and understanding of the customer's needs. By using strategies such as limited-time promotions, social proof, and follow-up techniques, you can increase the likelihood of making the sale and building a long-term relationship with the customer. Remember, the sale is just the beginning of a journey towards customer satisfaction and loyalty.

Chapter Five

Recruiting and Team Building
Building a team for your direct selling business

Direct selling can be a rewarding and profitable business, but it can also be challenging to build and maintain a successful team. As a direct seller, your income and success can greatly depend on the size and productivity of your team. Building a team can seem daunting, but with the right strategies and approach, it can be an achievable and rewarding goal.

One of the first steps in building a team for your direct selling business is to identify potential team members. Look for people who are enthusiastic about your product or service and who have a desire to build their own business. It can be helpful to reach out to friends and family members, but don't limit yourself to just your immediate circle. Consider attending networking events or using social media to connect with potential team members.

Once you have identified potential team members, it is important to provide them with the tools and support they need to succeed. This includes training, resources, and ongoing support. The more successful your team members are, the more successful your business will be.

Effective communication is also critical in building and maintaining a successful team. Make sure to keep your team members informed about new products, promotions, and training opportunities. Encourage open communication and be available to answer any questions or concerns they may have.

It is also important to set realistic goals for your team and provide incentives to motivate them to achieve those goals. This can include bonuses, trips, or recognition within the company. Celebrate the successes of your team members and acknowledge their hard work and dedication.

As your team grows, it can be challenging to manage and keep track of everyone's progress. This is where technology can be a valuable tool. Use a customer relationship management (CRM) system to manage your team's progress, track sales, and provide training and resources.

Another key to building a successful team is to lead by example. Show your team members what it takes to be successful in direct selling by consistently working hard, following up with customers, and staying up-to-date on product knowledge and industry trends. Your team will look to you for guidance and inspiration, so it's important to set a positive and motivated tone.

In addition to building a team, it's also important to focus on retaining team members. This includes providing ongoing support, recognizing their accomplishments, and creating a positive team culture. Make sure to listen to your team members' feedback and address any concerns they may have.

Encourage a supportive and collaborative environment where team members can learn from each other and grow together.

Finally, don't forget to have fun! Building a team can be a challenging process, but it's important to enjoy the journey and celebrate the successes along the way. Host team events, attend conferences together, and encourage your team members to get to know each other outside of work. The stronger the relationships within your team, the more successful your business will be.

In conclusion, building a team for your direct selling business requires time, effort, and dedication. But with the right strategies and approach, it can be a rewarding and profitable endeavor. Focus on identifying potential team members, providing them with the tools and support they need, and leading by example. Remember to celebrate successes, create a positive team culture, and have fun along the way. With a strong team in place, the sky's the limit for your direct selling business.

Effective recruiting techniques

Recruiting is an essential aspect of any direct selling business. A direct selling business heavily relies on the number of people working for it to achieve growth and success. Without effective recruiting techniques, businesses may struggle to grow and expand their customer base, as well as the sales force. In this article, we will explore some effective recruiting techniques that can help you build a strong team for your direct selling business.

1. Identify your target audience

The first step in effective recruiting is identifying your target audience. Who is your ideal candidate? What qualities do they possess? What motivates them? Identifying your target audience will help you craft a message that resonates with them and helps you find the right people for your team.

2. Leverage your existing network
   One of the most effective ways to recruit new team members is to leverage your existing network. Reach out to friends, family members, and colleagues who may be interested in joining your business. Offer them an incentive for joining, such as a discount on products or a bonus for hitting sales goals.

3. Attend events and network
   Attending events and networking is another effective way to recruit new team members. Attend industry events, trade shows, and conferences where you can meet like-minded individuals who may be interested in joining your business. Be prepared with business cards and information about your business to hand out to potential recruits.

4. Utilize social media
   Social media platforms like Facebook, Instagram, and LinkedIn are great tools for recruiting new team members. You can post about your business and share success stories to attract potential recruits. You can also create a Facebook group for your team members where you can share training materials, tips, and other helpful resources.

5. Offer training and support
    Offering training and support to your team members is crucial in retaining them. Provide them with the resources they need to succeed, such as product information, sales scripts, and training materials. Schedule regular check-ins with your team members to provide feedback and support.

6. Be transparent
    Be transparent with your team members about the requirements and expectations of the business. Let them know what is expected of them in terms of sales goals, time commitment, and other requirements. Being transparent will help you build trust with your team members and ensure that everyone is on the same page.

7. Provide incentives and rewards
    Providing incentives and rewards for hitting sales goals and recruiting new team members can be a powerful motivator. Offer bonuses, prizes, and other incentives to keep your team members engaged and motivated. This will also help to build a sense of community and camaraderie among your team members.

Effective recruiting techniques are essential to building a successful team for your direct selling business. Identify your target audience, leverage your existing network, attend events and network, utilize social media, offer training and support, be transparent, and provide incentives and rewards. By following these techniques, you can attract the right people to your team and help your business achieve its goals. Remember, building a strong team takes time and effort, but it is worth it in the end.

Motivating and training your team

In direct selling, building and maintaining a motivated and trained team is essential to the success of your business. Your team members are not just sellers of your products but also representatives of your company's brand, and it's important to ensure that they are equipped with the skills and knowledge they need to be successful.

One of the first steps to motivate your team is to create a positive and supportive work environment. Encourage open communication and create a culture where team members can voice their concerns and share their ideas freely. Provide feedback and recognition for a job well done, and address any issues that arise promptly and professionally.

Training is also crucial for the success of your team. Make sure your team members receive thorough training on your products, sales techniques, and customer service. Provide ongoing training opportunities to help your team members stay up-to-date on industry trends and new product offerings. This will help them to better serve your customers and increase sales.

In addition to training, it's important to set clear and achievable goals for your team. This will help them to stay focused and motivated, and give them a sense of direction and purpose.

Encourage them to set their own personal goals as well, and support them in achieving those goals.

Another effective way to motivate your team is to provide incentives and rewards for achieving their goals. This can be anything from a bonus or commission to a company-sponsored trip or event. Incentives and rewards not only motivate your team to work harder and sell more, but also foster a sense of camaraderie and teamwork.

Regular team meetings and communication are also important to keep your team motivated and informed. Use these opportunities to discuss progress toward goals, address any issues, and share best practices. Encourage your team members to share their own experiences and successes, and use these as teaching moments for the rest of the team.

Lastly, lead by example. As a leader of your direct selling team, your behavior and attitude will set the tone for the rest of the team. Be positive, enthusiastic, and passionate about your products and your business. Show your team that you are committed to their success and are willing to work alongside them to achieve their goals.

Building a motivated and trained team is a critical aspect of direct selling success. Creating a positive and supportive work environment, providing thorough training and ongoing education, setting clear and achievable goals, offering incentives and rewards, regular communication, and leading by example are all effective ways to motivate and train your team.

By investing in your team, you are investing in the long-term success of your direct selling business.

Chapter Six

Time Management and Productivity
Managing your time effectively

Managing your time effectively is crucial when it comes to direct selling. Time management can mean the difference between a thriving business and one that struggles to stay afloat. As a direct seller, you wear many hats, and juggling all the responsibilities can be overwhelming. However, with effective time management skills, you can maximize your productivity, minimize stress, and achieve your goals.

The first step in managing your time effectively is to prioritize your tasks. Make a to-do list of all the things you need to accomplish in a day, a week, or a month, and then rank them in order of importance. Focus on the most important tasks first, and then work your way down the list. By completing the most important tasks first, you ensure that the critical aspects of your business are taken care of.

Another way to manage your time effectively is to set realistic goals. Identify what you want to achieve and set a timeline for achieving it. Break down your goals into smaller, manageable tasks that you can work on every day. Celebrate the small wins along the way, as they will keep you motivated and help you track your progress.

Eliminating distractions is also essential to managing your time effectively. It is easy to get sidetracked when working from home or in a busy environment. Identify the things that distract you the most, and take steps to minimize them. For instance, turn off your phone, email notifications, and social media while working on important tasks. Set boundaries and let your friends and family know that you are not available during certain hours of the day.

In addition to minimizing distractions, creating a routine can also help you manage your time effectively. Establish a regular work schedule and stick to it as much as possible. Set aside time for specific tasks, such as marketing, sales, and training, and allocate a specific amount of time for each task. This helps you stay on track and ensures that you are making progress towards your goals.

Delegate tasks to others if possible. As your business grows, it becomes increasingly difficult to do everything yourself. Consider outsourcing tasks such as bookkeeping, social media management, or customer service to others. This will free up your time to focus on the critical aspects of your business.

Finally, it is essential to take breaks and practice self-care. Overworking yourself can lead to burnout and negatively impact your productivity. Take breaks throughout the day to recharge and refocus your energy. Take care of your physical and mental health by eating well, exercising regularly, and getting enough sleep.

Managing your time effectively is crucial to the success of your direct selling business. Prioritize your tasks, set realistic goals, eliminate distractions, establish a routine, delegate tasks, and take care of yourself. By following these strategies, you can maximize your productivity, minimize stress, and achieve your goals.

Prioritizing tasks and setting goals

Time management is one of the key skills necessary for success in any field, and direct selling is no exception. As a direct seller, you have to juggle various tasks, from prospecting and selling to team building and training, all while keeping an eye on your goals. Prioritizing tasks and setting goals can help you stay on track and achieve success in your direct selling business.

First and foremost, it's essential to set clear and specific goals for your business. These goals can be short-term or long-term, and they should be realistic, measurable, and achievable. When setting your goals, consider the amount of time and effort you can realistically dedicate to your business, as well as your financial goals and personal aspirations. Once you have a clear idea of your goals, break them down into smaller, actionable steps that you can take to achieve them.

Prioritizing tasks is also crucial to managing your time effectively. You'll have many tasks to complete each day, and it's essential to determine which tasks are most important and require immediate attention. One way to prioritize tasks is to use a time management matrix, which categorizes tasks based on their urgency and importance. Tasks that are urgent and important should be tackled first, followed by those that are important but not urgent. Tasks that are urgent but not important can be delegated to others, while those that are neither urgent nor important should be eliminated or postponed.

Another way to prioritize tasks is to focus on the activities that generate the most income or have the most significant impact on your business. For example, if you're a direct seller for a skincare company, you might prioritize activities that generate sales, such as prospecting and follow-up with customers. Alternatively, if you're focused on team building, you might prioritize activities that support your team's growth and development, such as training and mentoring.

It's also essential to manage your time effectively by creating a schedule and sticking to it as much as possible. A schedule helps you stay on track and ensures that you have enough time for all the tasks that need to be done. It's also helpful to set boundaries and avoid distractions, such as social media or other non-work-related activities, during your designated work hours.

In addition to prioritizing tasks and setting goals, it's important to regularly review your progress and make adjustments as needed. You may need to adjust your goals or re-prioritize tasks based on changes in your business or personal life. Regularly assessing your progress also helps you identify areas where you can improve and make necessary changes to achieve success.

Finally, it's important to practice self-care and take breaks as needed. Burnout is a common issue in direct selling and can negatively impact your productivity and effectiveness. Taking breaks, practicing stress-management techniques, and prioritizing self-care activities can help you maintain your motivation and focus on achieving your goals.

In conclusion, prioritizing tasks and setting goals are essential to managing your time effectively as a direct seller. By setting clear and specific goals, prioritizing tasks, creating a schedule, and regularly reviewing your progress, you can stay on track and achieve success in your direct selling business. Remember to practice self-care and take breaks as needed to avoid burnout and maintain your motivation. With these strategies in place, you can effectively manage your time and achieve your goals as a direct seller.

Maximizing productivity and avoiding burnout

In today's fast-paced and competitive world, many of us are constantly striving to be more productive, to achieve more, and to succeed in our personal and professional lives. As a direct seller, it's even more important to be productive, efficient, and effective in order to build and grow your business. However, it's also important to avoid burnout, which can have serious consequences for both your business and your personal life. In this chapter, we'll explore some strategies for maximizing your productivity while avoiding burnout.

One of the keys to maximizing productivity is to identify and prioritize your most important tasks. This means being clear about what your goals are, and focusing on the tasks that will help you achieve those goals. One helpful strategy is to use a task list or planner, where you can track your daily and weekly tasks, and organize them by priority. This can help you stay focused and avoid getting sidetracked by less important tasks.

Another important strategy for maximizing productivity is to avoid multitasking. While many of us believe that multitasking can help us get more done in less time, research has shown that multitasking can actually reduce our productivity and increase our stress levels. Instead, try to focus on one task at a time, and give it your full attention until it's completed.

In addition to prioritizing your tasks and avoiding multitasking, it's also important to take breaks and recharge your batteries. Research has shown that taking breaks can actually increase our productivity and creativity, as well as reduce our stress levels. One effective strategy is to use the Pomodoro technique, where you work for a set period of time (usually 25 minutes) and then take a short break (usually 5 minutes). After four Pomodoro cycles, take a longer break (usually 15-20 minutes) to recharge.

Another important factor in maximizing productivity and avoiding burnout is self-care. This means taking care of yourself physically, mentally, and emotionally. This includes getting enough sleep, eating a healthy diet, exercising regularly, and practicing stress-reducing activities like meditation or yoga. When you take care of yourself, you're better able to manage stress, stay focused, and be productive.

Finally, it's important to set boundaries and manage your time effectively. As a direct seller, it's easy to fall into the trap of working all hours of the day and night, and never really disconnecting from your business. However, this can quickly lead to burnout and can have negative consequences for your personal life as well. To avoid this, set clear boundaries around your work hours, and make sure to take time off to recharge and spend time with family and friends. Additionally, make sure to manage your time effectively by setting realistic goals and deadlines, and by delegating tasks to others when appropriate.

Maximizing productivity and avoiding burnout are critical for success in direct selling. By identifying and prioritizing your most important tasks, avoiding multitasking, taking breaks and practicing self-care, setting boundaries, and managing your time effectively, you can build a successful business without sacrificing your well-being. Remember, a healthy and balanced life is key to long-term success and happiness.

Chapter Seven

Networking and Building Your Customer Base
Building a customer base through networking

In the world of direct selling, networking is everything. You cannot simply sit back and wait for customers to come to you. You have to be proactive and put yourself out there, meet new people, and make connections. This is where networking comes in. Networking involves building relationships with other people, and in the world of direct selling, these relationships can be incredibly valuable.

One of the most important aspects of networking is being able to communicate effectively. You need to be able to introduce yourself, talk about your business, and answer questions in a way that is clear and concise. You also need to be able to listen to what other people have to say and respond appropriately. This is why it is important to practice your communication skills and be confident in what you are saying.

Another important aspect of networking is being able to find the right people to talk to. You want to target individuals who may be interested in your products or services, or who may know others who are. This means attending events where your target market is likely to be, such as trade shows, conferences, and community events. You can also join groups and associations that are relevant to your business, such as local chambers of commerce or business networking groups.

Once you have identified potential customers or contacts, it is important to follow up with them. This means exchanging contact information and keeping in touch. You can do this by sending emails, making phone calls, or even sending handwritten notes. The goal is to stay on their radar and build a relationship with them over time.

It is also important to remember that networking is a two-way street. You need to be willing to help others as well. This can mean introducing them to other people, sharing your expertise or resources, or simply offering a listening ear. By being generous and helpful, you will build goodwill and strengthen your relationships with others.

Another effective way to build a customer base through networking is by hosting events. This can be anything from a small gathering at your home to a larger event at a rented venue. The key is to make it fun and engaging, and to provide value to your guests. This could mean offering product demonstrations, hosting a workshop or class, or providing entertainment or refreshments. By hosting events, you can showcase your products and services, meet new people, and build relationships with potential customers.

Finally, social media is another powerful tool for networking and building a customer base. Platforms like Facebook, Instagram, and LinkedIn allow you to connect with people all over the world, and share your message with a wider audience.

You can use these platforms to promote your business, share valuable content, and engage with your followers. You can also join groups and communities on these platforms that are relevant to your business, and connect with like-minded individuals.

Building a customer base through networking is an essential part of direct selling. By being proactive, communicating effectively, and building relationships with others, you can grow your business and achieve success. So get out there, attend events, join groups, and start making connections. You never know where your next customer or business partner may come from.

Finding and connecting with potential customers

As a direct seller, your success is largely determined by your ability to find and connect with potential customers. But in today's world where people are constantly bombarded with advertisements, social media posts, and emails, it can be challenging to stand out and reach your target audience. However, with some effective strategies, you can find and connect with potential customers and build a strong customer base for your direct selling business.

The first step in finding and connecting with potential customers is to identify your target audience. Who are the people that would be interested in your products or services? What are their needs, interests, and pain points? Once you have a clear understanding of your target audience, you can start to develop a strategy to reach them.

One of the most effective ways to find and connect with potential customers is through networking. Attend local events, such as trade shows, community fairs, and networking events, and make sure to have your business cards, samples, and brochures with you. Be approachable, and strike up conversations with people who seem interested in your products or services. Exchange contact information and follow up with them after the event.

Another great way to connect with potential customers is through social media. With billions of people using social media platforms like Facebook, Instagram, and Twitter, social media can be a powerful tool for reaching your target audience. Create a business page for your direct selling business, and post regularly with engaging content that showcases your products or services. Use hashtags and tags to increase your visibility, and engage with your followers by responding to their comments and messages.

Email marketing is another effective strategy for finding and connecting with potential customers. Build an email list of people who have expressed interest in your products or services, and send them regular emails with information, promotions, and updates about your business. Make sure your emails are visually appealing, and include a clear call-to-action that encourages recipients to take action, such as visiting your website or making a purchase.

Referral marketing is also a great way to find and connect with potential customers. Encourage your satisfied customers to refer their friends and family to your business, and offer incentives such as discounts or free products for every new customer they refer. Word-of-mouth marketing can be incredibly powerful, and referrals from satisfied customers can help you build a strong customer base.

When connecting with potential customers, it's important to be genuine and build a relationship with them. Focus on their needs and interests, and provide value through your interactions. Don't be pushy or aggressive in your sales approach, and always follow up in a timely manner.

In addition to these strategies, it's also important to track your results and make adjustments as needed. Use analytics tools to monitor the effectiveness of your marketing campaigns, and adjust your strategy based on what is working and what isn't.

Finding and connecting with potential customers can be a challenge, but with the right strategies and mindset, you can build a strong customer base for your direct selling business. By networking, leveraging social media, using email marketing, and focusing on referral marketing, you can reach your target audience and build lasting relationships with your customers.

Maintaining customer relationships and retaining loyal customers

As a direct seller, building and maintaining strong relationships with your customers is crucial for the success of your business. It is much easier to retain loyal customers than to constantly seek new ones, which is why customer relationship management (CRM) should be an essential part of your business strategy. In this article, we will discuss some tips for maintaining customer relationships and retaining loyal customers.

1. Follow up regularly: After making a sale, follow up with your customer to ensure they are satisfied with the product or service. This shows that you care about their experience and want to make sure they are happy with their purchase. It also opens up an opportunity for you to address any issues or concerns they may have.

2. Offer exceptional customer service: Providing exceptional customer service can set you apart from your competitors and can make a big difference in retaining loyal customers. Responding to queries promptly, resolving complaints quickly, and going the extra mile to meet their needs can help build trust and loyalty.

3. Show appreciation: Show your customers that you appreciate their business by offering special promotions or discounts exclusively to them. Small gestures like sending a thank-you note or a personalized gift can also go a long way in building a strong relationship.

4. Keep in touch: Stay in touch with your customers by sending regular updates about your products or services. This can be in the form of a monthly newsletter, email updates, or social media posts. Keeping them informed about new products, promotions, and industry news can

help build a sense of community and keep your business top of mind.

5. Personalize your approach: Every customer is unique, so it's important to personalize your approach. Take the time to get to know your customers and their needs. This will help you tailor your products or services to meet their specific requirements, which can lead to higher satisfaction and increased loyalty.

6. Ask for feedback: Asking for feedback shows that you value your customers' opinions and are committed to improving their experience. Encourage your customers to provide feedback on their experience with your product or service and use this feedback to improve your offerings.

7. Offer loyalty programs: Implementing a loyalty program can be an effective way to retain customers and build loyalty. Offer rewards such as exclusive discounts, free products, or personalized offers to customers who make repeat purchases.

8. Address complaints promptly: Addressing complaints promptly can help turn a negative experience into a positive one. Take the time to listen to your customers' concerns and work to resolve the issue quickly and effectively.

9. Show your expertise: Sharing your knowledge and expertise with your customers can help build trust and credibility. Provide helpful tips, advice, and insights about your industry, products, or services. This can be in the form of blog posts, social media content, or in-person consultations.

10. Be consistent: Consistency is key in building and maintaining customer relationships. Make sure you deliver on your promises and provide a consistent experience across all touchpoints. This will help build trust and reliability with your customers.

In conclusion, building and maintaining strong customer relationships is essential for the success of your direct selling business. By following these tips, you can retain loyal customers, build trust and credibility, and differentiate yourself from your competitors. Remember that happy customers are your best advocates, so focus on providing exceptional customer service and delivering value at every opportunity.

Chapter Eight

Online and Social Media Marketing
Understanding the role of online and social media marketing in direct selling

The world of business has undergone a massive transformation in recent years with the advent of the internet and social media. Direct selling, in particular, has been significantly impacted by these changes. Today, online and social media marketing play a vital role in the success of any direct selling business. In this article, we will take a closer look at the role of online and social media marketing in direct selling.

The first thing to understand is that online marketing is no longer optional for any business, including direct selling. In fact, it is a must-have tool in the marketing arsenal of any business today. Online marketing offers a variety of options, including social media marketing, email marketing, pay-per-click advertising, search engine optimization, and more.

Social media marketing, in particular, has become an essential tool for direct sellers. Platforms like Facebook, Instagram, Twitter, and LinkedIn provide direct sellers with an excellent opportunity to connect with potential customers and build a strong brand presence. Social media marketing offers the following benefits:

1. Increased Reach: Social media platforms have billions of active users, and direct sellers can use these platforms to connect with potential customers who may not have been reachable through traditional marketing channels.

2. Cost-Effective: Social media marketing is a cost-effective way to promote products and services, particularly for direct sellers who may have limited marketing budgets.

3. Customer Engagement: Social media platforms offer a unique opportunity to engage with customers and build a relationship with them. Direct sellers can respond to customer queries and feedback, provide product information, and share their brand story with their followers.

4. Brand Awareness: Social media marketing helps in building brand awareness by creating a strong online presence. Direct sellers can use social media to showcase their products, post customer testimonials and reviews, and share their success stories with their followers.

Apart from social media, email marketing is another popular tool used by direct sellers. Email marketing helps in reaching out to potential customers directly and offers the following benefits:

1. Personalization: Email marketing allows direct sellers to personalize their messages and offers to target specific customers.

2. Cost-Effective: Email marketing is a cost-effective way to reach out to potential customers and promote products and services.

3. Measurable: Email marketing offers the ability to track open rates, click-through rates, and conversion rates, making it easy to measure the success of a campaign.

In addition to online and social media marketing, direct sellers must also ensure that they have a robust website that is optimized for search engines. Search engine optimization (SEO) helps direct sellers to appear on the top pages of search engines like Google and Bing, making it easier for potential customers to find their business.

The role of online and social media marketing in direct selling cannot be overstated. Social media marketing, email marketing, and search engine optimization offer direct sellers an opportunity to reach out to potential customers, build a strong brand presence, and engage with customers. By incorporating these strategies into their marketing plan, direct sellers can increase their customer base and drive sales.

Creating a strong online presence for your business

In today's world, having a strong online presence is essential for the success of any business, including direct selling businesses. The internet and social media platforms have revolutionized the way businesses interact with customers and reach out to new audiences. Having a strong online presence can not only help you connect with customers in real-time, but it can also help you build brand recognition and credibility. Here are some tips for creating a strong online presence for your direct selling business:

1. Develop a Website: Creating a website is a crucial step in building a strong online presence for your business. A website is the central hub where customers can find information about your business, products, and services. It should be visually appealing, easy to navigate, and optimized for search engines. Make sure to include your contact information and links to your social media profiles to make it easy for customers to connect with you.

2. Utilize Social Media Platforms: Social media platforms like Facebook, Instagram, and Twitter offer a powerful way to connect with customers and build relationships. Use social media to share updates about your business, new products, and promotions. Engage with your followers by responding to comments and messages, and regularly posting content that is relevant and interesting to your target audience.

3. Create Valuable Content: Creating valuable content is essential for building a strong online presence. Share content that is informative and relevant to your target audience. This can include blog posts, videos, infographics, and more. Your content should be educational, engaging, and focused on providing value to your customers.

4. Implement SEO Strategies: Search engine optimization (SEO) is a critical component of building a strong online presence. SEO involves optimizing your website and content to rank higher in search engine results pages. Research and use relevant keywords and phrases in your website content and meta descriptions to increase visibility and attract more traffic.

5. Leverage Email Marketing: Email marketing is a powerful tool for building relationships with customers and driving sales. Collect email addresses from your customers and use an email marketing platform to send newsletters, promotions, and updates about your business.

6. Monitor Online Reputation: It's essential to monitor your online reputation and respond to customer feedback promptly. Encourage customers to leave reviews on platforms like Google, Facebook, and Yelp, and respond to both positive and negative reviews. This demonstrates that you value customer feedback and are committed to providing excellent customer service.

7. With Influencers: Partnering with influencers can be a great way to reach new audiences and build brand awareness. Identify influencers in your niche who have a significant following and engage with them on social media. Offer them free products or services in exchange for promoting your business to their followers.

In conclusion, building a strong online presence is essential for the success of any direct selling business. By following these tips, you can create a powerful online presence that helps you connect with customers, build brand recognition, and drive sales. Remember to focus on providing value to your customers and engaging with them regularly to build long-lasting relationships.

Utilizing social media to grow your business

In today's world, social media has become an integral part of our lives, and it has also become an essential tool for businesses to connect with their customers. Social media provides a platform for businesses to reach out to potential customers, build their brand, and engage with their existing customers. Direct sellers can utilize social media to grow their business and reach a wider audience.

To effectively use social media for direct selling, it's important to understand the different platforms available and how to use them. Facebook, Instagram, Twitter, LinkedIn, and YouTube are some of the most popular social media platforms used for direct selling. Each platform has its own strengths and weaknesses, so it's important to choose the ones that work best for your business.

To create a strong social media presence for your business, it's important to start with a clear strategy. This strategy should define your target audience, your goals, and the type of content you will be posting. Your strategy should also include a plan for how you will engage with your audience and how often you will post.

One of the keys to success on social media is consistency. It's important to post regularly and to maintain a consistent tone and style across all your platforms. This helps to establish your brand and build trust with your audience.

Another important aspect of social media is engagement. Social media is a two-way conversation, and it's important to engage with your audience by responding to comments, answering questions, and addressing concerns. This helps to build relationships and establish trust with your audience.

One effective way to grow your business on social media is to leverage the power of influencers. Influencers are people who have a large following on social media and can help to promote your products or services to their audience. When choosing an influencer, it's important to look for someone who aligns with your brand and target audience.

Social media also provides a great opportunity to showcase your products or services. By posting high-quality photos and videos, you can highlight the benefits and features of your products and show potential customers how they can benefit from using them.

Another way to grow your business on social media is to run targeted ads. Platforms like Facebook and Instagram allow you to target specific demographics, interests, and behaviors, so you can reach the right people with your ads.

In conclusion, social media is a powerful tool that can help direct sellers grow their business and reach a wider audience. By understanding the different platforms available and how to use them effectively, direct sellers can create a strong online presence, engage with their audience, and ultimately drive sales and grow their business.

Chapter Nine

Overcoming Obstacles and Challenges in Direct Selling

Common obstacles and challenges faced by direct sellers

Direct selling can be a lucrative and rewarding business opportunity, but it also comes with its fair share of challenges and obstacles. As a direct seller, you may encounter various challenges that can hinder your success and progress in the industry. Understanding these obstacles and how to overcome them is essential to building a successful direct selling business.

One of the common challenges faced by direct sellers is the perception of the industry itself. Many people still hold negative stereotypes and misconceptions about direct selling, which can make it difficult to recruit new customers and team members. It's important to address these misconceptions and educate people about the benefits and legitimacy of direct selling.

Another common challenge is competition. With so many direct selling companies out there, it can be challenging to differentiate yourself and stand out in the market. It's important to identify your unique selling proposition and focus on delivering value to your customers and team members.

Managing time is also a challenge for many direct sellers. Balancing the demands of running a business with personal responsibilities can be overwhelming and stressful. It's important to prioritize tasks and set realistic goals to make the most of your time and avoid burnout.

Another obstacle faced by direct sellers is rejection. Rejection is a natural part of the sales process, but it can still be discouraging and demotivating. It's important to develop resilience and the ability to bounce back from rejection by focusing on your goals and learning from your experiences.

Compliance with regulations and laws is also a challenge for direct sellers. There are many laws and regulations that direct sellers must comply with, including those related to product claims, income disclosures, and taxes. Failure to comply with these regulations can lead to legal and financial consequences, so it's important to stay informed and up-to-date on the latest regulations.

Recruiting and retaining team members is another challenge faced by many direct sellers. Building a team is essential to growing your business, but it can be challenging to find and retain the right people. It's important to develop effective recruiting strategies and provide ongoing training and support to help your team members succeed.

Finally, technology can also pose a challenge for direct sellers. With the rise of e-commerce and social media, it's important to stay current with the latest technology and trends in online marketing. This can be challenging for those who are not tech-savvy, but it's essential to embrace technology and use it to your advantage to grow your business.

Direct selling comes with its fair share of obstacles and challenges, but with the right mindset and strategies, they can be overcome. It's important to stay informed, focused, and resilient in the face of challenges and to always be learning and growing as a direct seller. By doing so, you can build a successful and rewarding direct selling business that can provide you with financial freedom and flexibility.

Strategies for overcoming these challenges

Direct selling is an industry that is full of opportunities, but it is not without its challenges. There are many obstacles that direct sellers may face, from competition to rejection to burnout. However, with the right mindset and strategies in place, these challenges can be overcome. In this article, we will explore some common obstacles and challenges faced by direct sellers, and some strategies for overcoming them.

One of the biggest challenges faced by direct sellers is competition. With so many companies and products available, it can be difficult to stand out and attract customers. One strategy for overcoming this challenge is to focus on building relationships with customers. By providing excellent customer service and personalized attention, direct sellers can build a loyal customer base that will continue to purchase products and refer others. Another strategy is to differentiate oneself from competitors by offering unique products or services, or by specializing in a particular niche.

Rejection is another common obstacle that direct sellers face. Not everyone will be interested in purchasing products or joining the business opportunity, and it can be discouraging to face rejection. One strategy for overcoming this challenge is to focus on the positives and reframe rejection as an opportunity for growth. Direct sellers can use rejection as a learning experience, asking for feedback and using it to improve their approach. It can also be helpful to have a strong support system, such as a team or mentor, who can provide encouragement and guidance during challenging times.

Another challenge faced by direct sellers is burnout. It can be easy to get caught up in the excitement of building a business and working long hours, but this can lead to exhaustion and burnout. To overcome this challenge, it is important to prioritize self-care and set boundaries. Direct sellers should take breaks when needed, prioritize rest and relaxation, and ensure that they are not sacrificing their personal relationships or health for the sake of their business. It can also be helpful to have a clear schedule and to prioritize tasks based on their importance.

One final challenge that direct sellers may face is legal and ethical issues. Direct selling is a heavily regulated industry, and it is important for direct sellers to understand the laws and regulations that apply to their business. This includes issues such as income claims, product claims, and proper compensation of team members. One strategy for overcoming this challenge is to educate oneself on the relevant laws and regulations, and to ensure that one's business practices are in compliance. It can also be helpful to seek out legal or professional advice when needed.

Direct selling is a challenging but rewarding industry, and there are many strategies that can be used to overcome obstacles and challenges. By focusing on building relationships with customers, reframing rejection as an opportunity for growth, prioritizing self-care and setting boundaries, and staying informed on legal and ethical issues, direct sellers can build successful businesses that bring value to themselves and their customers.

Building resilience and perseverance in direct selling

Direct selling can be a challenging career, and as with any business venture, there are bound to be setbacks along the way. In order to succeed in direct selling, it's important to build resilience and perseverance. This means developing the ability to bounce back from failure, maintain motivation during difficult times, and stay focused on long-term goals.

One of the first steps to building resilience and perseverance in direct selling is to develop a positive mindset. Direct sellers who are able to maintain a positive outlook, even during difficult times, are more likely to be successful in the long run. This means focusing on the possibilities instead of the obstacles, and maintaining a strong belief in oneself and one's abilities.

Another key factor in building resilience and perseverance is the ability to adapt to change. Direct selling is an ever-changing industry, and successful direct sellers are those who are able to stay ahead of the curve and adapt to new trends and technologies. This may mean being open to trying new marketing strategies, staying up-to-date on the latest industry news and developments, and being willing to pivot when necessary.

In addition to a positive mindset and adaptability, building resilience and perseverance in direct selling also requires a strong work ethic. Direct selling is not a "get rich quick" scheme, and those who are willing to put in the time and effort required to build a successful business are more likely to succeed. This means setting clear goals and working consistently towards them, even when progress may seem slow or setbacks occur.

Direct sellers who are able to build strong relationships with their customers and team members are also more likely to be resilient and persevere through difficult times. This means taking the time to understand the needs and preferences of each customer, and building genuine connections with them. It also means investing in the growth and development of one's team members, and creating a supportive and encouraging work environment.

When setbacks do occur, it's important for direct sellers to take a proactive approach to problem-solving. This means identifying the root cause of the problem, and coming up with a plan to address it. It may also mean seeking out the advice and support of other successful direct sellers, and learning from their experiences.

Finally, building resilience and perseverance in direct selling also requires a willingness to learn and grow. Successful direct sellers are those who are always seeking out new knowledge and skills, and who are constantly striving to improve themselves and their businesses. This means staying up-to-date on the latest industry trends, attending training events and conferences, and investing in one's own personal and professional development.

Building resilience and perseverance is a critical component of success in direct selling. It requires a positive mindset, adaptability, a strong work ethic, a focus on building relationships, proactive problem-solving, and a commitment to ongoing learning and growth. By cultivating these qualities, direct sellers can overcome obstacles, stay motivated during difficult times, and ultimately achieve their goals.

Chapter Ten

Managing Finances and Taxes
Managing finances and budgeting for your business

One of the keys to success in direct selling is effectively managing your finances and budgeting for your business. While it may not be the most glamorous aspect of running your own business, it is essential to keep track of your income, expenses, and profits in order to make informed decisions and maximize your earning potential.

The first step in managing your finances is to keep accurate records of all your transactions. This means keeping track of all the money coming in and going out of your business, whether it's through sales, expenses, or investments. You can use accounting software, spreadsheets, or even a simple notebook to keep track of your financial data.

Once you have an accurate record of your finances, you can start to create a budget for your business. A budget is a plan that outlines your expected income and expenses for a specific period of time, usually a month or a year. By creating a budget, you can identify areas where you may need to cut back on spending, as well as areas where you can invest more to help grow your business.

When creating your budget, it's important to be realistic about your income and expenses. Don't overestimate your sales or underestimate your expenses, as this can lead to unrealistic expectations and financial stress. Be sure to include all of your fixed expenses, such as rent, utilities, and insurance, as well as your variable expenses, such as advertising and marketing costs.

Another important aspect of managing your finances is monitoring your cash flow. Cash flow refers to the amount of money that is coming in and going out of your business on a regular basis. It's important to have a positive cash flow in order to pay your bills on time, invest in your business, and maintain a healthy financial position.

To manage your cash flow effectively, you can create a cash flow statement that outlines your expected inflows and outflows for a specific period of time. This can help you identify potential cash shortages and take steps to address them before they become a problem.

In addition to managing your finances on a day-to-day basis, it's important to plan for the long-term financial health of your business. This includes saving for taxes, investing in your business, and creating a retirement plan for yourself.

When it comes to taxes, it's important to set aside a portion of your income to cover your tax obligations. This can help you avoid a financial shock when tax season comes around, and ensure that you're in compliance with all tax laws and regulations.

Investing in your business can also help you grow and succeed over the long term. This can include investing in new products, marketing campaigns, or training programs for yourself or your team. By investing in your business, you can increase your earning potential and create a sustainable source of income.

Finally, creating a retirement plan for yourself can help ensure your long-term financial security. This can include setting up a savings account or retirement plan, such as an IRA or 401(k), and regularly contributing to it. By planning ahead for your retirement, you can create a financial cushion that will allow you to enjoy the fruits of your labor for years to come.

Managing your finances and budgeting for your business is an essential part of direct selling success. By keeping accurate records, creating a realistic budget, monitoring your cash flow, planning for taxes and investments, and creating a retirement plan, you can build a strong financial foundation for your business and achieve your financial goals.

Understanding tax laws and regulations for direct sellers

As a direct seller, it's important to understand the tax laws and regulations that apply to your business. Failing to comply with these laws can lead to penalties, fines, and even legal issues. Therefore, it's crucial to have a good understanding of the tax requirements that apply to you as a direct seller.

The first thing you need to understand is that as a direct seller, you are essentially operating your own business. This means that you will need to keep accurate records of your income and expenses, just like any other business owner. You will also need to file your taxes with the relevant government agency, typically the Internal Revenue Service (IRS) in the United States.

One important tax requirement for direct sellers is to obtain a Tax Identification Number (TIN) from the IRS. This is a unique number that is used to identify your business for tax purposes. You can apply for a TIN online through the IRS website, or by filling out a paper application.

Another important tax consideration for direct sellers is the classification of your income. In the United States, direct selling income is typically considered self-employment income. This means that you will be responsible for paying self-employment taxes, which include both Social Security and Medicare taxes. It's important to keep accurate records of your income and expenses so that you can properly calculate your self-employment tax liability.

In addition to self-employment taxes, you may also be required to pay state and local sales taxes on the products you sell. These requirements can vary by state and locality, so it's important to understand the rules in your area. Some states have specific sales tax requirements for direct sellers, while others may require you to register for a sales tax permit or collect and remit sales tax on your own.

Finally, it's important to keep good records of your business expenses so that you can take advantage of deductions on your tax return. Common business expenses for direct sellers may include travel expenses, office supplies, and advertising costs. These expenses can be deducted from your income, which can help to reduce your overall tax liability.

Understanding tax laws and regulations is an important aspect of running a successful direct selling business. By obtaining a TIN, properly classifying your income, paying self-employment taxes, complying with state and local sales tax requirements, and keeping accurate records of your business expenses, you can ensure that you are meeting your tax obligations and minimizing your tax liability. It's a good idea to consult with a tax professional who is knowledgeable about direct selling to ensure that you are following all of the rules and regulations that apply to your business. With proper planning and preparation, you can build a successful and profitable direct selling business while staying in compliance with all applicable tax laws and regulations.

Keeping financial records and tracking expenses

When it comes to running a direct selling business, keeping track of your finances and expenses is crucial for success. Not only is it important for tax purposes, but it also allows you to monitor your business's financial health and make informed decisions about future investments and growth opportunities. In this chapter, we will explore the importance of keeping financial records and provide some tips and strategies for effectively tracking expenses.

First and foremost, it is essential to keep accurate and up-to-date financial records. This includes recording all sales, expenses, and other financial transactions in a clear and organized manner. One way to do this is by using accounting software, such as QuickBooks or Xero, which can help you automate your record-keeping process and generate financial reports. Alternatively, you can keep track of your finances using spreadsheets or a ledger book, as long as you ensure that all information is recorded accurately and regularly.

It is also important to separate your personal and business finances. This means having a separate bank account and credit card for your direct selling business, and using these accounts solely for business-related transactions. This will make it easier to track your expenses and ensure that you are not mixing personal and business finances, which can create confusion and potentially lead to tax issues.

In addition to keeping accurate records, it is important to track your expenses regularly. This means recording every expense, no matter how small, and categorizing them appropriately. Common expense categories for direct sellers include:

- Product costs: This includes the cost of purchasing products from your direct selling company, as well as any shipping or handling fees.
- Marketing and advertising: This includes any expenses related to promoting your business, such as Facebook ads or business cards.

- Home office expenses: This includes expenses related to your home office, such as rent, utilities, and internet fees.
- Travel expenses: This includes any expenses related to traveling for business purposes, such as gas, tolls, and hotel costs.

By tracking your expenses in these categories, you can get a clear picture of where your money is going and identify areas where you may be overspending. This can help you make more informed decisions about budgeting and planning for the future.

Another important aspect of tracking expenses is keeping receipts and other supporting documentation. This can include invoices, bank statements, and credit card receipts. By keeping these records, you can easily verify your expenses if you are audited by the IRS or need to provide documentation for tax purposes.

In addition to tracking expenses, it is important to regularly review your financial statements and reports. This can include your income statement, balance sheet, and cash flow statement. By analyzing these reports, you can identify trends and patterns in your business's financial performance, and make informed decisions about where to allocate your resources.

Finally, it is important to stay up-to-date on tax laws and regulations for direct sellers. This includes understanding the deductions and credits available to you as a business owner, as well as any reporting requirements and deadlines. It is also important to keep accurate records of all your financial transactions and to work with a tax professional to ensure that you are compliant with all applicable laws and regulations.

Keeping accurate financial records and tracking expenses is crucial for success as a direct seller. By separating your personal and business finances, tracking expenses regularly, and staying up-to-date on tax laws and regulations, you can make informed decisions about budgeting, planning, and investing in your business's future.

Chapter Eleven

Goal Setting and Measuring Success
Setting and achieving goals for your direct selling business

Setting and achieving goals is a critical component of success in direct selling. Without clear objectives and a plan for achieving them, a direct seller can easily become lost and directionless. In this chapter, we will explore the importance of setting goals and strategies for achieving them.

Firstly, it is essential to understand the difference between a goal and a dream. A goal is a specific, measurable, achievable, realistic, and time-bound objective that you can work towards. In contrast, a dream is a vague, unrealistic, and often unattainable idea that lacks a clear plan for achieving it. To achieve success in direct selling, you must set clear, actionable goals that align with your values and vision.

When setting goals for your direct selling business, it is essential to begin with the end in mind. What do you want to achieve in the long-term? Once you have a clear vision, you can break it down into smaller, achievable goals. These smaller goals should be specific, measurable, and have a deadline. For example, instead of setting a goal to "increase sales," set a specific goal to "increase sales by 10% in the next quarter."

To achieve your goals, you must have a plan for achieving them. This plan should include specific actions that you will take to achieve each goal, as well as a timeline for completing them. Your plan should also include strategies for overcoming obstacles and challenges that may arise along the way.

It is also essential to track your progress towards your goals regularly. This will help you stay focused and motivated, as well as provide insight into areas where you may need to make adjustments. By monitoring your progress, you can identify what is working well and what needs improvement.

In addition to setting and achieving goals for your direct selling business, it is also important to celebrate your achievements along the way. Celebrating your successes will help you stay motivated and provide a sense of accomplishment that will encourage you to continue striving towards your goals.

One effective strategy for setting and achieving goals in direct selling is to use the SMART framework. This framework involves setting goals that are Specific, Measurable, Achievable, Realistic, and Time-bound. By setting goals that meet these criteria, you increase your chances of success and avoid becoming overwhelmed by unrealistic or unattainable objectives.

Another effective strategy is to break your goals down into smaller, more manageable steps. This will help you stay focused and motivated, as well as provide a sense of progress towards your larger goals. By breaking your goals down into smaller steps, you can also identify areas where you may need to make adjustments and course-correct along the way.

Setting and achieving goals is a critical component of success in direct selling. By setting clear, actionable objectives and developing a plan for achieving them, you can stay focused, motivated, and on track towards achieving your vision for your business. Remember to celebrate your successes along the way, and don't be afraid to adjust your course as needed to ensure you stay on track towards achieving your goals. With dedication, perseverance, and a clear vision, you can achieve success in direct selling and build a profitable and fulfilling business.

Measuring success and tracking progress

Success is a subjective term, and it can mean different things to different people. However, in direct selling, measuring success and tracking progress is essential to achieving your goals and growing your business. It helps you stay focused, motivated, and on track, and it allows you to make informed decisions about your business strategies.

Measuring success and tracking progress in direct selling can be done in a variety of ways. Here are some of the most common methods:

1. Sales Volume: The most obvious way to measure success in direct selling is by tracking your sales volume. You can set a sales target for a specific period, say a month or a quarter, and then track your progress towards that

target. This can give you a clear idea of how much you're selling and whether you're on track to achieve your goals.

2. Customer Base: Another important metric for measuring success in direct selling is your customer base. You can track the number of customers you have, their average order value, and their purchase frequency. This will give you an idea of how loyal your customers are and how much they are contributing to your overall sales.

3. Recruiting: In direct selling, recruiting new members to your team is critical to growing your business. You can measure your success in recruiting by tracking the number of new team members you bring on board and how successful they are in making sales and recruiting others.

4. Social Media Engagement: In today's digital age, social media plays a crucial role in direct selling. You can measure your success in social media engagement by tracking the number of followers you have, your engagement rate, and your conversion rate. This will help you understand how effective your social media marketing efforts are and how much they are contributing to your overall sales.

5. Personal Development: Success in direct selling isn't just about making sales and growing your team. It's also about personal development and growth. You can measure your success in personal development by tracking the skills you've acquired, the books you've

read, and the training you've attended. This will help you understand how much you're growing as a person and how much that growth is contributing to your overall success.

Once you've identified the metrics you want to track, the next step is to set goals for each of them. Your goals should be specific, measurable, achievable, relevant, and time-bound. For example, if your goal is to increase your sales volume by 20% in the next quarter, you should break that down into specific actions you can take, such as increasing the number of customer interactions or offering a new product line.

It's also essential to regularly review and analyze your progress towards your goals. This will help you identify what's working and what's not, and allow you to make adjustments to your strategies accordingly. If you're not meeting your goals, don't get discouraged. Instead, take the opportunity to learn from your mistakes and make changes to your approach.

In conclusion, measuring success and tracking progress in direct selling is crucial to achieving your goals and growing your business. By identifying the metrics you want to track, setting specific and achievable goals, and regularly reviewing your progress, you can stay on track and make informed decisions about your business strategies. Remember, success in direct selling isn't just about making sales and growing your team; it's also about personal growth and development. So don't forget to measure your progress in these areas as well.

Celebrating achievements and learning from failures

Celebrating achievements and learning from failures are two sides of the same coin when it comes to direct selling. Success is not only about achieving goals but also about taking the time to appreciate the progress you've made and the hard work you've put in. On the other hand, failures and setbacks are inevitable in any business, but they provide valuable opportunities to learn, grow, and improve. In this chapter, we will explore the importance of celebrating achievements and learning from failures in direct selling.

First, let's talk about celebrating achievements. When you reach a milestone or achieve a goal, it's essential to take the time to celebrate your accomplishment. Celebrating achievements not only provides a sense of satisfaction and motivation, but it also helps you reflect on your progress and the hard work you've put in to get where you are. Celebrating your successes can come in many forms, from treating yourself to something special to sharing your achievements with others. It's essential to acknowledge and appreciate the effort you've put in, no matter how small the accomplishment may seem.

However, it's equally important to learn from failures. In direct selling, setbacks and failures are a part of the process. The key is not to dwell on them but to use them as opportunities to learn and improve. When you experience a setback, take the time to reflect on what went wrong, what you could have done differently, and what you can do to avoid similar mistakes in the future. Failure is not a reason to give up; it's a chance to learn and grow. By embracing failures and using them as a learning opportunity, you can improve your skills and strategies, and ultimately achieve greater success.

It's also important to remember that success and failure are not black and white. In direct selling, success can be measured in many ways, from achieving sales targets to building a strong team to improving your personal skills. Similarly, failures are not always clear-cut; they can be minor setbacks or significant obstacles. It's essential to recognize and celebrate progress, no matter how small, and to learn from setbacks, no matter how minor.

One way to celebrate achievements and learn from failures is to track your progress and set goals for yourself. By setting specific, measurable, achievable, relevant, and time-bound (SMART) goals, you can track your progress and hold yourself accountable for achieving them. Celebrating your successes and learning from failures becomes more manageable when you have a clear understanding of what you're working towards and where you stand in achieving those goals.

It's also important to share your successes and failures with others in your direct selling network. Celebrating your accomplishments with your team and fellow direct sellers can create a sense of community and motivation, while sharing your failures can help others learn from your experiences and avoid similar mistakes. In addition, seeking feedback from others can provide valuable insights into your strengths and weaknesses and help you improve your skills and strategies.

Celebrating achievements and learning from failures are essential components of success in direct selling. Taking the time to acknowledge and appreciate your successes can provide a sense of satisfaction and motivation, while embracing failures as opportunities to learn and grow can help you improve your skills and strategies. By setting goals, tracking your progress, sharing your experiences with others, and embracing both successes and failures, you can achieve greater success in direct selling and beyond.

Chapter Twelve

Personal Development and Leadership
The role of personal development in direct selling

Personal development is an essential aspect of direct selling. It is a process that helps direct sellers acquire new skills, knowledge, and attitudes that they can apply to improve their performance and achieve their goals. Personal development can help direct sellers develop a growth mindset, increase their self-awareness, and improve their interpersonal skills. In this article, we'll explore the role of personal development in direct selling and how it can help direct sellers achieve success.

One of the key benefits of personal development in direct selling is that it can help direct sellers develop a growth mindset. A growth mindset is the belief that one's abilities and qualities can be developed through dedication and hard work. Direct sellers who have a growth mindset are more likely to persist through challenges and setbacks, as they see them as opportunities to learn and grow. This mindset is especially important in direct selling, where rejection and failure are common. By embracing a growth mindset, direct sellers can improve their resilience and increase their chances of success.

Another benefit of personal development in direct selling is that it can help direct sellers increase their self-awareness. Self-awareness is the ability to recognize one's own thoughts, feelings, and behaviors, and how they affect others. Direct sellers who have high levels of self-awareness can better understand their strengths and weaknesses and how they impact their performance. This knowledge can help them identify areas where they need to improve and seek out opportunities for growth and development.

Personal development can also help direct sellers improve their interpersonal skills. Interpersonal skills are the abilities that people use to interact with others. They include communication skills, listening skills, empathy, and the ability to build rapport. These skills are critical in direct selling, where the ability to connect with customers and build relationships is essential. Direct sellers who have strong interpersonal skills can create a positive customer experience, which can lead to increased sales and referrals.

Direct sellers can engage in personal development in a variety of ways. One common approach is to attend training and development programs offered by their direct selling company. These programs can provide direct sellers with the knowledge and skills they need to succeed in their business. Another approach is to read books, listen to podcasts, or attend seminars on personal development. These resources can help direct sellers develop new perspectives and gain insights into how to improve their performance.

In addition to these formal approaches, direct sellers can also engage in informal personal development activities. These might include seeking out feedback from customers and colleagues, reflecting on their experiences and what they've learned, or seeking out mentorship from more experienced direct sellers. These informal activities can help direct sellers gain a deeper understanding of themselves and their business and identify areas where they can improve.

Personal development is an essential aspect of direct selling. It can help direct sellers develop a growth mindset, increase their self-awareness, and improve their interpersonal skills. Direct sellers who engage in personal development are more likely to succeed in their business, as they are better equipped to handle challenges and adapt to changes in the market. By investing in their personal development, direct sellers can achieve greater success and fulfillment in their business and their lives.

Developing leadership skills as a direct seller

As a direct seller, developing leadership skills is crucial to your success in the business. Being a leader means taking charge, setting an example, and inspiring others to follow in your footsteps. Direct selling requires a certain level of confidence and charisma that can only be enhanced by strong leadership skills.

To begin developing your leadership skills, start by setting a vision for your direct selling business. A vision is a clear picture of what you want to achieve and what your business will look like in the future. It should be specific, measurable, achievable, relevant, and time-bound (SMART). Once you have a vision, you can begin to set goals and develop strategies to achieve them.

Communication is another essential component of effective leadership. As a direct seller, you must be able to communicate effectively with your team, customers, and potential customers. This means being able to listen actively, speak clearly and confidently, and provide feedback in a constructive manner. It also means being able to inspire and motivate others with your words and actions.

Another important aspect of leadership is the ability to delegate tasks and responsibilities. Delegating allows you to focus on the most important aspects of your business while also empowering your team members to take ownership of their work. It also helps to build trust and respect among team members, which is essential for a strong and cohesive team.

In addition to delegation, effective leadership also requires coaching and mentoring. This means providing guidance and support to team members to help them develop their skills and reach their full potential. Coaching and mentoring can take many forms, such as providing feedback, sharing knowledge and experience, and offering encouragement and motivation.

A strong leader also understands the importance of continuous learning and development. This means seeking out new knowledge and skills, attending training and development programs, and staying up-to-date with industry trends and best practices. By investing in your own development, you can become a more effective leader and inspire others to do the same.

Finally, a strong leader leads by example. This means modeling the behaviors and values that you want to see in your team members and customers. It also means being transparent and accountable for your actions and decisions. By demonstrating integrity, honesty, and a strong work ethic, you can build trust and inspire loyalty among your team members and customers.

Developing leadership skills is essential for success in direct selling. By setting a vision, communicating effectively, delegating tasks, coaching and mentoring, investing in continuous learning and development, and leading by example, you can become an effective and inspiring leader in your business. Remember that leadership is not a one-time achievement, but a continuous process of growth and development. With persistence and dedication, you can become the kind of leader that inspires and motivates others to reach their full potential.

Building a personal brand and reputation

Building a personal brand and reputation is crucial for success in direct selling. As a direct seller, you are not only promoting the products or services you sell, but you are also selling yourself as a trusted and reliable source of information and guidance. Building a strong personal brand can help you establish yourself as an authority in your field and attract loyal customers and team members.

Here are some tips for building a strong personal brand in direct selling:

1. Define your brand identity: Start by defining who you are as a person and what you stand for. What are your values and beliefs? What are your unique strengths and skills? Use this information to develop your brand identity and messaging.

2. Be consistent: Consistency is key to building a strong personal brand. Use the same profile picture, bio, and messaging across all your social media platforms and other marketing materials. This will help create a sense of familiarity and trust with your audience.

3. Be authentic: Authenticity is important in direct selling. Be honest about your experiences and your journey. Share your successes and failures, and be transparent about your motivations and goals.

4. Provide value: One of the best ways to build your personal brand is to provide value to your audience. Share helpful tips, information, and insights related to your products or services. Answer questions and provide guidance to your followers.

5. Build relationships: Building relationships is at the heart of direct selling. Take the time to connect with your followers and customers on a personal level. Show that you care about their needs and concerns, and provide personalized recommendations and solutions.

6. Develop a unique selling proposition: A unique selling proposition (USP) is a statement that defines what sets you apart from your competition. Develop a USP that highlights your unique strengths and the value you bring to your customers.

7. Invest in your personal development: Personal development is essential for building a strong personal brand. Take the time to invest in yourself by attending workshops, reading books, and seeking out mentorship opportunities. This will not only help you grow as a person but also help you develop new skills and knowledge that can benefit your business.

8. Seek out endorsements and recommendations: Positive endorsements and recommendations from satisfied customers and team members can go a long way in building your personal brand and reputation. Encourage your customers and team members to leave reviews and testimonials on your website or social media pages.

Building a strong personal brand takes time and effort, but it is well worth it in the long run. By defining your brand identity, being consistent and authentic, providing value, building relationships, developing a unique selling proposition, investing in your personal development, and seeking out endorsements and recommendations, you can establish yourself as a trusted and respected authority in the world of direct selling.

Chapter Thirteen

Ethics and Compliance in Direct Selling
Understanding ethical standards in direct selling

Direct selling is a business model that relies heavily on the trust and confidence of customers. This trust is built on the foundation of ethical standards and practices in direct selling. As a direct seller, understanding and following ethical standards is not only essential to building a successful business, but it is also necessary for the integrity and reputation of the entire industry.

One of the most important ethical standards in direct selling is honesty. Direct sellers must be honest with their customers about the products they are selling, the benefits of those products, and any potential risks or side effects. This includes being truthful about the ingredients, performance, and limitations of products. Honesty also extends to the sales process, where direct sellers should be transparent about pricing, shipping costs, and any applicable taxes or fees.

Another key ethical standard in direct selling is respect. Direct sellers should treat their customers, team members, and colleagues with respect and professionalism. This includes being attentive to their needs, providing excellent customer service, and responding promptly to any questions or concerns.

Direct sellers should also respect the privacy of their customers and protect their personal information.

In addition to honesty and respect, direct sellers must also adhere to the ethical standard of fairness. This includes treating all customers and team members fairly, regardless of their race, gender, age, or other personal characteristics. Direct sellers should also avoid any practices that may be perceived as unfair or deceptive, such as making false or exaggerated claims about the benefits of products.

Another important ethical standard in direct selling is responsibility. Direct sellers are responsible for the products they sell, as well as the claims they make about those products. This includes ensuring that products are safe and meet any applicable regulatory requirements. Direct sellers should also take responsibility for their own actions and behavior, including ensuring that they comply with all applicable laws and regulations.

Direct sellers must also adhere to the ethical standard of integrity. This means being honest and transparent in all their dealings, and acting with integrity even when no one is watching. Direct sellers should also avoid any practices that may be perceived as unethical, such as engaging in deceptive advertising or making false or misleading claims about the benefits of products.

Finally, direct sellers should prioritize the ethical standard of trust. Trust is the foundation of any successful direct selling business, and direct sellers must work hard to earn and maintain the trust of their customers and team members. This includes being transparent and honest in all their dealings, responding promptly to any concerns or complaints, and ensuring that they follow through on any promises or commitments they make.

In conclusion, ethical standards play a crucial role in direct selling, and direct sellers must be committed to upholding these standards at all times. By following ethical practices, direct sellers can build strong relationships with their customers and team members, and contribute to the growth and success of the entire direct selling industry. Ultimately, ethical standards are not just good business practices, but they are also necessary for the long-term sustainability and reputation of the industry.

Compliance with laws and regulations

Compliance with laws and regulations is a critical component of any business operation, including direct selling. As a direct seller, it is important to be aware of the legal requirements that apply to your business and ensure that you are conducting your business in accordance with the law. Failure to comply with these laws and regulations can result in legal liability and reputational damage to your business.

One of the primary legal requirements for direct selling businesses is to have a clear and transparent compensation plan. Your compensation plan must be easily understandable by your sales force and must accurately reflect the commissions and bonuses that they are entitled to receive. Additionally, your compensation plan must comply with all relevant laws and regulations, including those related to minimum wage and overtime pay.

Another important area of compliance for direct selling businesses is consumer protection. Direct sellers must ensure that their marketing and advertising materials are truthful and not misleading. Any claims made about the products or services being sold must be backed up by reliable evidence. Additionally, direct sellers must provide accurate information about the product or service being sold, including any risks or potential side effects.

Direct sellers must also comply with data protection laws. This includes protecting the personal information of customers and sales representatives, as well as ensuring that any personal data is collected and used in accordance with applicable laws and regulations. Direct sellers must also ensure that any data collected is kept secure and protected from unauthorized access or use.

Tax compliance is another important area for direct sellers. As a direct seller, you are responsible for paying all relevant taxes, including income tax and sales tax. You must ensure that you are properly registered with the relevant tax authorities and that you are filing your tax returns in a timely and accurate manner.

In addition to these legal requirements, direct sellers must also comply with any industry-specific regulations or guidelines. For example, some countries have specific regulations governing direct selling, such as requirements for registration or limitations on the types of products that can be sold.

To ensure compliance with all relevant laws and regulations, it is important for direct sellers to stay up-to-date on any changes or updates to the legal landscape. This may involve working with legal counsel or regulatory experts to understand the requirements that apply to your business and ensure that you are in compliance.

In addition to avoiding legal liability and reputational damage, compliance with laws and regulations can also benefit your business in other ways. For example, it can help to build trust with your customers and sales representatives, as they will have confidence that your business is operating in a responsible and ethical manner. Compliance can also help to promote a positive image for your business and differentiate you from competitors who may not be operating in accordance with the law.

In summary, compliance with laws and regulations is essential for any direct selling business. As a direct seller, it is important to be aware of the legal requirements that apply to your business and take steps to ensure that you are conducting your business in compliance with those requirements. By doing so, you can help to protect your business from legal liability, build trust with your customers and sales representatives, and promote a positive image for your business.

Building a trustworthy and ethical business

Building a trustworthy and ethical business is not only a moral responsibility but also a vital component for long-term success in the direct selling industry. Trust and integrity are the pillars on which any business is built, and it is crucial to establish a strong foundation of ethics from the very beginning.

One of the keys to building a trustworthy and ethical business is to have a clear set of values and principles that guide every decision and action. These values should be reflected in every aspect of the business, from the products and services offered to the way in which the business is marketed and sold. By establishing a strong set of ethical guidelines, a business can ensure that it is operating in an honest and transparent manner.

Another important aspect of building a trustworthy and ethical business is to maintain open lines of communication with customers, team members, and other stakeholders. This means being transparent about business practices and making an effort to address any concerns or complaints in a timely and effective manner. By demonstrating a commitment to transparency and accountability, a business can build a strong reputation and establish trust with customers and team members.

One way to maintain transparency and accountability is to regularly review and evaluate the business's compliance with laws and regulations. This includes everything from product safety and labeling requirements to tax laws and labor regulations. By staying up to date on compliance issues, a business can avoid legal trouble and maintain a reputation for ethical business practices.

In addition to legal compliance, it is also important to consider the social and environmental impact of the business. This includes issues such as sustainability, human rights, and fair labor practices. By taking a proactive approach to these issues and implementing policies that prioritize social and environmental responsibility, a business can demonstrate a commitment to ethical practices and build a reputation as a socially responsible company.

Building a trustworthy and ethical business also involves being mindful of potential conflicts of interest and taking steps to avoid them. This includes avoiding situations where personal or financial gain may conflict with the interests of customers or team members. It also means being transparent about any potential conflicts of interest and taking steps to mitigate them.

Finally, building a trustworthy and ethical business involves taking responsibility for mistakes and taking steps to make things right. This means acknowledging mistakes and taking steps to address any harm caused. By demonstrating a commitment to accountability and making a genuine effort to right wrongs, a business can build trust and demonstrate a commitment to ethical practices.

Building a trustworthy and ethical business is a crucial component of success in the direct selling industry. By establishing a strong set of values and principles, maintaining transparency and accountability, staying up to date on legal and regulatory compliance, prioritizing social and environmental responsibility, avoiding conflicts of interest, and taking responsibility for mistakes, a business can build a reputation as an ethical and trustworthy company. This not only benefits the business in the short term but also helps to build a loyal customer base and establish a foundation for long-term success.

Chapter Fourteen

International Direct Selling and Cultural Differences

Understanding cultural differences in international direct selling

Direct selling is a global business, and as such, it is important for direct sellers to understand and respect cultural differences in order to succeed in international markets. Cultural differences can affect everything from business practices to communication styles, and it is crucial for direct sellers to take the time to learn about these differences and adapt accordingly.

One of the most important things to understand about cultural differences is that they can have a significant impact on business practices. For example, in some cultures, it is considered impolite to negotiate aggressively, while in others, it is expected. In some cultures, it is common to build relationships through gift-giving, while in others, it may be seen as bribery. Direct sellers who are not familiar with these cultural norms may unintentionally offend potential customers or partners and damage their business relationships.

In addition to business practices, communication styles can also vary widely between cultures. For example, some cultures may value direct and assertive communication, while others may prefer a more indirect and polite approach. Direct sellers who are not aware of these differences may unintentionally come across as rude or pushy, or they may miss important cues that could help them build stronger relationships.

Another important aspect of understanding cultural differences in direct selling is recognizing that different cultures may have different expectations and priorities when it comes to product features and benefits. Direct sellers may need to adapt their marketing and sales strategies to meet the unique needs and preferences of customers in different regions. This may involve modifying product packaging, adjusting marketing messaging, or even offering different products altogether.

One way that direct sellers can build cultural competence is by doing their research. This may involve reading books or articles about different cultures, attending cultural events or festivals, or even working with a cultural consultant who can provide insights and guidance. Direct sellers should also take the time to listen and learn from their customers and partners in different regions, and be open to feedback and suggestions.

Another important strategy for building cultural competence is to be humble and open-minded. Direct sellers who approach new cultures with a sense of curiosity and a willingness to learn are more likely to succeed than those who assume that their way of doing things is the only right way. By recognizing and respecting cultural differences, direct sellers can build strong, lasting relationships with customers and partners around the world.

Finally, it is important for direct sellers to remember that cultural differences are not just a challenge to be overcome, but also an opportunity for growth and learning. By embracing and celebrating diversity, direct sellers can broaden their perspectives, expand their networks, and develop new skills that will benefit them both personally and professionally.

Understanding cultural differences is an essential part of succeeding in international direct selling. Direct sellers who take the time to learn about different cultures, adapt their business practices and communication styles, and embrace diversity and inclusivity are more likely to build strong, successful businesses that can thrive in any market around the world.

Adapting to different cultural practices and customs

When you are conducting international direct selling, it is essential to be aware of cultural differences in business practices and customs. Every culture has its unique norms, beliefs, and values that can impact the way people do business. Adapting to these differences can help you build trust with your customers and create successful business relationships. Here are some tips for adapting to different cultural practices and customs in international direct selling.

Do Your Research

Before entering a new market, it is important to do your research and understand the local culture. This includes studying business practices, customs, and communication styles. You can do this by reading books and articles, attending cultural training programs, or consulting with local experts.

This knowledge will help you avoid cultural missteps and build trust with your potential customers.

Respect Local Customs

In many cultures, business relationships are built on personal relationships. This means that it is important to take the time to build rapport with your customers before trying to sell them something. In some cultures, it is also customary to bring a small gift when meeting someone for the first time. Taking the time to learn about and respect these customs can go a long way in building trust with your potential customers.

Communication is Key

Communication is an essential aspect of doing business in any culture. However, communication styles can vary greatly from one culture to another. For example, in some cultures, it is considered rude to be direct when giving feedback or saying no to a request. In other cultures, being direct is preferred. It is important to understand these differences and adapt your communication style accordingly. It is also important to be aware of non-verbal communication, such as body language and tone of voice, which can convey different meanings in different cultures.

Be Flexible

When doing business in a new culture, it is important to be flexible and adaptable. Things may not always go according to plan, and it is important to be able to adjust your approach as needed. This includes being willing to negotiate and compromise on certain aspects of your business to better align with local customs and practices.

Build Local Partnerships

Building partnerships with local businesses and organizations can be a great way to navigate cultural differences in international direct selling. Local partners can provide valuable insights into the local culture and help you navigate business practices and customs. They can also help you build trust with potential customers by vouching for your business and products.

In conclusion, understanding and adapting to cultural differences in international direct selling is essential for building successful business relationships. By doing your research, respecting local customs, adapting your communication style, being flexible, and building local partnerships, you can navigate cultural differences with ease and build trust with your customers.

Building a global direct selling business

Building a global direct selling business can be a daunting task, but it is also an exciting opportunity to expand your reach and increase your sales potential. With the rise of e-commerce and the increasing demand for convenient shopping experiences, direct selling businesses have the potential to thrive in the global marketplace. However, there are also unique challenges that come with operating in a global environment, such as navigating different cultural practices, languages, and regulations.

To build a successful global direct selling business, it's important to first do your research and gain an understanding of the different markets you plan to operate in. This includes identifying potential customers, competitors, and cultural practices that may impact your business. Consider partnering with local distributors who have a strong understanding of the market and can help you navigate any cultural or regulatory barriers.

One key aspect of building a global direct selling business is developing a strong online presence. This means creating a website that is accessible to customers in different languages and currencies, as well as utilizing social media platforms that are popular in the markets you plan to enter. It's important to tailor your marketing strategy to the specific needs and preferences of each market, rather than simply replicating what works in your home market.

Another important consideration is logistics and shipping. When selling internationally, it's important to have a reliable and cost-effective shipping strategy in place. This may require working with different shipping carriers or utilizing third-party logistics providers who have experience in international shipping and customs clearance.

In addition to logistical challenges, it's important to be aware of any legal and regulatory requirements for operating a direct selling business in different countries. This includes compliance with local tax laws, licensing requirements, and other regulations that may vary from country to country. Consider working with legal professionals who have experience in international business law to ensure compliance and minimize risk.

When building a global direct selling business, it's also important to consider the cultural differences that may impact your business. This includes differences in language, customs, and social norms. Take the time to learn about the cultural practices of each market and tailor your marketing and sales strategies accordingly. This may include adjusting product offerings or marketing messaging to better resonate with local consumers.

Finally, building a global direct selling business requires a strong commitment to customer service and satisfaction. This means offering high-quality products, responsive customer service, and clear communication with customers in different time zones and languages. It's also important to build a strong reputation for your business by consistently delivering on your promises and treating customers with respect and fairness.

In summary, building a successful global direct selling business requires careful planning, research, and execution. By developing a strong online presence, navigating logistics and shipping challenges, complying with legal and regulatory requirements, and adapting to cultural differences, you can build a thriving business that reaches customers around the world. With a commitment to customer service and a strong reputation for ethical business practices, your global direct selling business has the potential to succeed and grow for years to come.

Conclusion

Recap of key concepts and strategies

As we come to the end of our journey exploring the world of direct selling, it is important to recap on the key concepts and strategies we have covered. Direct selling is a dynamic industry that provides many opportunities for individuals to build successful businesses. However, as we have learned, success in direct selling requires dedication, hard work, and a solid understanding of the key principles that underpin this industry.

One of the most important concepts we have explored is the importance of building strong relationships with customers. In direct selling, success is not just about making sales; it is about building long-lasting relationships with customers that go beyond the initial purchase. This means taking the time to understand your customers' needs and preferences, and delivering exceptional customer service that exceeds their expectations.

Another key concept we have explored is the importance of personal development in direct selling. To succeed in this industry, it is essential to develop strong leadership skills, as well as effective communication, time management, and goal-setting skills. By investing in personal development, direct sellers can improve their performance, build their confidence, and achieve their goals.

Building a strong personal brand and reputation is also critical to success in direct selling. This means establishing a clear brand identity that resonates with your target audience and aligns with your values. It also means consistently delivering on your promises and building a reputation for integrity, honesty, and transparency.

Ethical standards and compliance with laws and regulations are also key considerations in direct selling. By understanding the legal and ethical standards that apply to their business, direct sellers can ensure that they operate in a transparent and trustworthy manner. This means being aware of consumer protection laws, adhering to ethical business practices, and conducting their business in a way that is fair and honest.

When building a global direct selling business, it is essential to understand cultural differences and adapt to different practices and customs. This means taking the time to understand the cultural norms of the markets you operate in and adapting your sales and marketing strategies accordingly. By doing so, you can build strong relationships with customers and establish a successful business in new markets.

Finally, it is important to have a clear understanding of the key strategies that underpin success in direct selling. These include developing a strong product line, building a strong team of independent representatives, leveraging technology to streamline your operations, and investing in effective marketing and sales strategies.

As we conclude our journey through the world of direct selling, it is clear that success in this industry requires a comprehensive understanding of the key concepts and strategies that underpin this dynamic and fast-paced industry. By investing in personal development, building strong relationships with customers, adhering to ethical standards, and adapting to different cultural practices, direct sellers can build successful businesses that make a positive impact on the lives of their customers and communities.

Direct selling can be a highly rewarding career for those who are willing to put in the time and effort to build their business. It requires a unique set of skills and a strong entrepreneurial spirit to succeed in this industry. Throughout this series, we have covered a wide range of topics and strategies that can help direct sellers achieve success.

One of the key themes that has emerged throughout this series is the importance of building relationships. Whether it's with customers, team members, or colleagues, strong relationships are the foundation of a successful direct selling business. By putting the needs of others first and focusing on providing value to those around you, you can build a loyal following of customers and team members who will support you on your journey.

Another important concept that has been discussed is the need for ongoing personal development. As a direct seller, you are your own boss, and it's up to you to continually improve your skills and knowledge in order to stay ahead of the competition. This might involve investing in training programs, attending industry events, or working with a mentor who can help you identify areas for growth and improvement.

Of course, building a successful direct selling business also requires a strong work ethic and a commitment to consistent action. It's not enough to simply have a great product or a solid team - you need to be willing to put in the time and effort to promote your business, build your brand, and connect with potential customers and team members.

Finally, it's important to stay focused on your long-term goals and maintain a positive mindset. Building a successful direct selling business is not always easy, and there will be challenges and setbacks along the way. However, by staying focused on your vision and maintaining a positive attitude, you can overcome these obstacles and achieve the success you desire.

In conclusion, mastering direct selling requires a combination of skills, strategies, and mindset. By building strong relationships, investing in personal development, staying committed to consistent action, and maintaining a positive mindset, you can build a thriving direct selling business that brings you both financial and personal fulfillment. As you embark on your own direct selling journey, remember to stay focused on your goals, stay true to your values, and always be willing to learn and grow. With these key principles in mind, you can achieve success and make a meaningful impact in the lives of those around you.

Next steps for success in direct selling

Congratulations on completing this comprehensive guide on mastering direct selling! You now have a solid foundation for building a successful direct selling business. However, your journey does not end here. Direct selling is a dynamic and evolving industry, and you need to keep up with the latest trends and best practices to stay ahead of the competition.

So, what are the next steps for success in direct selling? Here are some suggestions to help you continue your journey:

1. Stay up-to-date with industry news and trends: Subscribe to industry publications, attend trade shows and conferences, and network with other direct sellers to stay informed about the latest trends and best practices in direct selling.

2. Continue your personal development: Direct selling requires strong leadership skills, self-discipline, and a positive mindset. Keep investing in your personal development through courses, books, and coaching to enhance your skills and mindset.

3. Leverage technology: Technology has revolutionized the direct selling industry, providing new ways to reach customers, track sales, and manage your business. Stay up-to-date with the latest technology trends and tools, and leverage them to streamline your business operations and improve your customer experience.

4. Expand your product line: Offering a diverse range of products can help you appeal to a wider customer base and increase your sales. Consider adding complementary products or partnering with other direct selling companies to expand your product line.

5. Build a team: As your business grows, you may want to consider building a team of direct sellers to help you reach more customers and increase your sales. Be selective in your recruiting process, and provide your team with the training and support they need to succeed.

6. Give back: Direct selling is not just about making money; it's also about making a positive impact on the world. Consider partnering with charitable organizations or participating in community service projects to give back to your community and enhance your brand reputation.

Remember, success in direct selling requires hard work, dedication, and a commitment to ongoing learning and improvement. But with the right mindset and strategies, you can achieve your goals and build a thriving business that brings value to your customers and enriches your life.

In conclusion, direct selling is a powerful and rewarding business model that offers limitless opportunities for growth and success. By following the strategies and best practices outlined in this guide, and continuing to learn and evolve, you can build a successful direct selling business that allows you to achieve your dreams and make a positive impact on the world. Good luck on your journey!

www.ingramcontent.com/pod-product-compliance
Lightning Source LLC
Chambersburg PA
CBHW072031230526
45466CB00020B/1434